T0067108

Personalized
Stress Relief
for Mind, Body, and Spirit

Linda L Boling

BALBOA
PRESS

A DIVISION OF HAY HOUSE

Balboa Press books may be ordered through booksellers or by contacting:

Balboa Press
A Division of Hay House
1663 Liberty Drive
Bloomington, IN 47403
www.balboapress.com
1 (877) 407-4847

Because of the dynamic nature of the Internet, any web addresses or links contained in this book may have changed since publication and may no longer be valid. The views expressed in this work are solely those of the author and do not necessarily reflect the views of the publisher, and the publisher hereby disclaims any responsibility for them.

The author of this book does not dispense medical advice or prescribe the use of any technique as a form of treatment for physical, emotional, or medical problems without the advice of a physician, either directly or indirectly. The intent of the author is only to offer information of a general nature to help you in your quest for emotional and spiritual well-being. In the event you use any of the information in this book for yourself, which is your constitutional right, the author and the publisher assume no responsibility for your actions.

Any people depicted in stock imagery provided by Thinkstock are models, and such images are being used for illustrative purposes only.
Certain stock imagery © Thinkstock.

Printed in the United States of America.

ISBN: 978-1-5043-2582-0 (sc)
ISBN: 978-1-5043-2584-4 (hc)
ISBN: 978-1-5043-2583-7 (e)

Library of Congress Control Number: 2014922995

Balboa Press rev. date: 02/05/2015

Contents

Introduction

Stress. It's everywhere and everyone has it. Stress isn't all bad and can actually be helpful – especially when you're about to be run down by a car! But it can also help motivate you to make a change. The problem is that most stress is an internal reaction that, basically, has nowhere to go. You come upon a situation that stresses you. Your body is ready to fight or run. You can't do either right then so you end up internalizing it instead. All the chemicals in your body that readied you to fight or run are just 'sitting there' affecting your mind, body and spirit.

There are lots of stress relief books out there. This book is different because it gives you specific anti-stress practices that will work for YOU. Using a combination of astrology and a self-test, you will find Mind, Body and Spirit practices that will lower your stress levels. Although information about stress is included, the point of this book to help you find some practices that will reduce or eliminate your stress levels.

Mind-Body-Spirit Personalized Stress Relief is broken into three parts. Part 1 is about stress, what it is, why you are stressed, and how stress affects your mind, body, and spirit. Part 2 includes a self-test and astrological information so you can determine what practices will work for you. Part 3 is a listing of all the stress relief practices by type: Mind, Body, and Spirit.

As always, check with your doctor before beginning any practices that may be contraindicated based on mental or physical issues. If your stress is extreme and debilitating, you need to see an expert, not a self-help book. Stress experts may be found in any of the following occupations- Psychologist, Psychotherapist, Nurse, and Physician.

A few facts about stress that you may not know:

- ❖ Two-thirds of office visits to a family doctor are for stress-related symptoms according to the American Academy of Family Physicians.
- ❖ In a recent poll, 89 percent of people said they had experienced serious stress in their lives.
- ❖ A recent study indicated that stress management programs may reduce the risk of heart problems, including heart attack, by up to 75 percent in people with heart disease.
- ❖ Stress-related mental disorders have been called the fastest growing occupational (work-related) disease in the U.S.

It's time to stop stressing! But, what is stress, exactly? Why do you get stressed? How does it affect your health – mind, body, and spirit? This section will answer those questions and more. It is important to learn how stress affects you, how to identify warning signs of stress, and how to find stress relievers that work for you.

Let's begin with what stress is according to you, me, and the experts…

PART 1

STRESS

What is Stress?

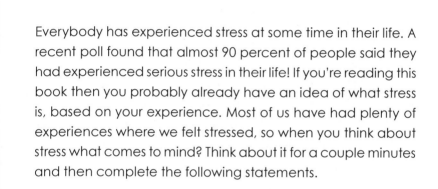

Everybody has experienced stress at some time in their life. A recent poll found that almost 90 percent of people said they had experienced serious stress in their life! If you're reading this book then you probably already have an idea of what stress is, based on your experience. Most of us have had plenty of experiences where we felt stressed, so when you think about stress what comes to mind? Think about it for a couple minutes and then complete the following statements.

Stress is...

Without stress, my life would be...

Okay, now you know how you feel about stress. But did you know that whatever you said, you're right!? Everyone has their own definition of stress. Whatever it is to you is just as valid as anyone else's idea of what stress is. Why? Because even the experts don't agree on what stress is. They can't even tell us its essential properties.

Stress is personal. What is stressful to one person may not be stressful to another. When the experts try to define stress, they keep coming back to that fact. It's not easy to determine something like stress when it depends on who you're asking!

Not only do we feel stress in different ways, but we can also adapt to stress. Studies have shown that with time and practice we can have the same experience but not feel as stressed by it the second, third or fourth time.

Think of a time when you were stressed. The first time going into a situation that stresses you is tough. But if you'd experienced the situation before, you have an idea of what may happen and that alone can make the situation less stressful.

Try to recall a stressful situation that you've had a few times. Try to remember what you felt the first time you experienced this situation and then how you felt the second, third or fourth time. For most people, the situation is less stressful the more you experience it.

Obviously, this 'adaptation' to a stressful situation makes it impossible to define stress for everyone. However, we all know when we're stressed and even if we're not really cognizant of it, our body most certainly is! We'll get more into the physical effects of stress in a bit but for now, let's continue attempting to define stress.

Using a medical model, the stress experts are able to come up with some ideas of what stress is. By measuring various physical properties and putting people in stressful or non-stressful situations, they have come up with some general definitions of stress.

According to Hans Selve (an endocrinologist who pioneered the study of stress in the 1930's) stress involves a stimulus and a response. This is a very common description of stress and is obviously based on a physical model. A stimulus is anything that a person encounters that creates a physical reaction that can be measured with various instruments.

A similar definition of stress by Herb Benson, M.D., defines stress as a combination of a stressor and a resulting stress reaction. He also includes the increasing stress levels for all of us due to our rapidly changing world. This definition clearly goes beyond just the physical effects of stress and is the most often used definition since it includes both physical and mental aspects of stress.

Experiencing a lot of change in a short period of time is highly stressful, as anyone who has experienced it can tell you. Not only is the body affected, but so is the mind. Often when you are very, very stressed, you find it hard to focus and think. Essentially, what is happening is that your resources are over-taxed and exceeding your resources and reserves. This is very serious stress and affects both the body and the mind.

Summing up, we could say the following is a general description of stress:

Stress occurs when an event is perceived to challenge one's resources or capability to respond. Therefore, stress is perceptual and is a function of how important the situation is perceived to the individual in personal terms and the extent to which individuals are not bothered by situations unimportant to them. In other words: stress is a physical and emotional way we respond to a perceived difficulty.

Why do you get stressed?

It's pretty much impossible to be alive and not get stressed at some time in your life. Any new situation can cause a bit of stress just because it is new. Most of us need some stress in our lives! No stress can lead you to boredom, lack of motivation and unfulfilled dreams and desires. Stress can be the one thing that gets us moving in a new and more powerful direction. Stress adds a bit of spice to our lives. It's when we have too much stress that we need to stop and do something to lessen it. The fast pace of today's world can create a lot of stress. Some examples of common stressful situations:

- You and your spouse both work full time while you are raising your family. At the same time, your parents are retired, in ill health, and are dependent on your help with shopping and running errands.
- You are a single person living alone, and your salary isn't rising as fast as the rate of inflation. It's getting harder each month to pay the bills.
- You are a divorced parent and share the custody of your children with your former spouse. But the friction between the two of you on matters concerning the children is becoming bitter and more frequent.
- The expectations and competition at your workplace is becoming fierce. You find yourself coming in early, staying late, and taking on more work than you can handle.

Some people are more likely to get stressed more than others. Why? There is an aspect of stress that is related to your personality. Are you someone who drives yourself harder than most people? Do you tend to take things very seriously? Are you impatient and unable sometimes to let things go? If so, you are probably more likely to feel stress.

Others are less likely to feel stressed. These folks are easy-going, take things as they come, and don't worry about the small stuff.

Can you change your personality? Yes, somewhat. If you are a stressor and worrier, you can learn to let things go. It's not something that will change overnight but if you work on it a bit every day, you can learn to be more relaxed and less worried. I know, because I have done it. Check out the Mind Practices section in Part 3 for some specific practices.

The chart below can also help you figure out what stresses you. For each statement:

> ➤ Check the box under 'Home' if the statement usually/mostly/always applies to you at home
> ➤ Check the box under 'Work' if it usually/mostly/always applies to you at work.
> ➤ If the statement rarely or never applies to you, leave the box empty.

Some questions may appear to apply more generally, but it is important to answer all questions in relation to both Home and Work. There are/is no right or wrong answers. There is no scoring.

	Statement	Home	Work
1	My motto is "If you can't do it perfectly, don't do it at all."		
2	I am not very good at telling people, "no".		
3	I expect people close to me to consider my feelings and needs as much as they do their own.		
4	I participate in physical activity for at least 30 minutes three times a week or more.		
5	I eat a balanced diet.		
6	When I feel pain in my body, I listen to it and try to relieve it.		
7	I have good friends and/or family to discuss my feelings with.		
8	When I feel stressed, I do something physical.		
9	I know how to breathe from my abdomen and do so regularly.		
10	I expect people to respect me.		
11	I am creative and imaginative.		
12	I laugh on a regular basis.		
13	I expect people to treat me fairly.		
14	Telling someone that I'm angry with him or her is okay.		
15	I have a lot of opportunities to express myself in positive ways.		
16	I feel that I have a good amount of control over what happens to me.		
17	I have people that listen to me and respect my opinions.		
18	Even though I don't show it, I like to win.		
19	I often compare myself to others in terms of accomplishments, income, performance, achievements, or value of property.		
20	I am aware of the time it takes to complete most things and am very rarely late for appointments.		
21	I am calm and take things as they come.		
22	I have a significant level of responsibility for others		
23	I am confident and not easily embarrassed when dealing with others.		

| 24 | I believe that I need to be in control of everything that happens to me. | | |
| 25 | I have a chronic illness, such as IBS, heart disease, ulcers, high blood pressure, or headaches. | | |

Certain occupations can also add stress to your life such as law enforcement and air traffic controller. Working in a job that you find boring or extremely difficult will also add stress. According to the Jobs Rated Almanac, the five most stressful jobs are:

1. President of the United States
2. Firefighter
3. Senior corporate executive
4. Race car driver
5. Taxi driver

Life events also play a major role in how stressed you are at any given time. Some life events whether positive or not, strongly affect your stress levels. In 1967 two psychiatrists, Thomas Holmes and Richard Rahe, examined medical records of over 5,000 patients to find out if there was a link between illness and a life stressor. Their results showed a definite correlation and subsequent research and testing validated what they had found. Their results were published and the scale has been used for years. It is most often referred to as the Holmes and Rahe Stress Scale.

To measure your stress according to the Holmes and Rahe Stress Scale:

Circle all the life events you have experienced in the last year and then add up all the circled numbers.

Personalized Stress Relief for Mind, Body, and Spirit

Life event	Life change units
Death of a spouse	100
Divorce	73
Marital separation	65
Imprisonment	63
Death of a close family member	63
Personal injury or illness	53
Marriage	50
Dismissal from work	47
Marital reconciliation	45
Retirement	45
Change in health of family member	44
Pregnancy	40
Sexual difficulties	39
Gain a new family member	39
Business readjustment	39
Change in financial status	38
Death of a close friend	37
Change to different line of work	36
Change in frequency of arguments	35
Major mortgage	32
Foreclosure of mortgage or loan	30
Change in responsibilities at work	29
Child leaving home	29
Trouble with in-laws	29
Outstanding personal achievement	28
Spouse starts or stops work	26
Beginning or end school	26
Change in living conditions	25
Revision of personal habits	24
Trouble with boss	23
Change in working hours or conditions	20
Change in residence	20
Change in schools	20
Change in recreation	19

Life event	Life change units
Change in church activities	19
Change in social activities	18
Minor mortgage or loan	17
Change in sleeping habits	16
Change in number of family reunions	15
Change in eating habits	15
Vacation	13
Christmas	12
Minor violation of law	11

Score of 300+: At risk of illness

Score of 150-299: Risk of illness is moderate.

Score <150: Slight risk of illness.

So, why do you get stressed? Thinking about what you've just read, make some notes about what you think increases your stress levels? Make notes here...

What is stress doing to your mind?

It's not always easy to split the mind and body when talking about stress. Things like burnout and anxiety are a combination of mind and body. However, for now we will look at the emotional, cognitive and behavioral changes that can be symptoms of too much stress.

Below is a list of some common symptoms of stress. How you respond to stress may include some of these emotional, cognitive and behavioral symptoms.

Emotional symptoms include:

❖ Tension
❖ Irritability
❖ Inability to concentrate

Cognitive symptoms include:

❖ Worrying
❖ Racing thoughts
❖ Being negative/pessimistic
❖ Poor judgment

Behavioral symptoms include:

- ❖ Procrastinating
- ❖ Avoiding daily responsibilities
- ❖ Increased use of alcohol, drugs, or cigarettes
- ❖ Isolation from friends and family

Your thoughts and emotions affect your behavior. If you are thinking about how much you dislike your job you will be less likely to want to do the work. The negative emotion of disliking your job shows up in how you behave when you have work to do.

When you are pessimistic about what is happening in your life, you find all the negatives are much bigger and more common than any positives. It is, indeed, a self-fulfilling prophecy.

When we view a situation as a 'problem' we create an emotional attachment to it. By thinking of the situation as a 'project' we release the emotional attachment and view it more clearly. Then we can see it more objectively and get clearer about our part in it. Once we can do that, we are on the way to changing ourselves and the situation so it will not continue to create stress for us.

Multitasking

It seems that these days everyone is required to multi-task. Job requirements often even include "Multitasker" as a requirement! The problem with multitasking is that it is not even possible. When you say you are multitasking, what you are really doing is switching from one thing to another very quickly.

Studies have shown that the human brain is simply not capable of focusing on more than one thing at a time. Every time you go from one thing to another you are simply changing focus rapidly, and doing so is adding to your stress levels. Your body actually produces stress hormones every time you switch from one thing to another. These stress hormones ultimately cause your mind to overload. When your mind is overloaded, it is easily distracted. In fact, the mind gets distracted on purpose – to allow it time to recover from the stress.

Multitasking may seem like a good idea, but clearly it is not. What you think is making you more efficient is actually making you LESS efficient. Your brain is wired to send stress hormones to your mind every time you try to multitask. It's simply the way the brain works. Give yourself a break and stop multitasking. You'll find that you have a lot less stress if you do!

From Problem to Project?

Every time you hear yourself saying, "I have a problem," stop, and change it to "I have a project to work on..." You will immediately release the emotionality of the situation and will feel calmer and clearer about it.

You may be someone who views new situations and stresses as a problem. It's easy to feel that a new stressor is just another problem you have to deal with. However, if you look at is as a *project* instead of a *problem* then you can remove the negative aspects of the stressor. When you see something as a project, you may not get excited about it but you can see it as something you have control of, and therefore can change. When you feel that you have the ability to change the situation, you are empowered. Indeed, you do have the power to change things. We all do. Once you've realized that you can change it, you can start thinking about how to change it. This shifts your mind from stressed to problem-solving and once you get there, you are on the way to less stress. There is a Mind Practice of Stress Journal in Part 3. As part of that practice, there is a section where you can write down the problem and some ideas you have to reduce the stressor.

Burnout

Burnout is a word used to describe the condition of people who have become discouraged, depressed, angry, or have developed a sense of helplessness about being able to alleviate stress and its sources. Another way to think of it is as the logical conclusion of stress over a long period of time.

The term burn suggests the anger, heat, or hostility of a person who strikes out at others. While some people *burn*, others are just *out* of it. They have nothing left. The person becomes uncommunicative and unable to understand his or her own feelings. Friends may say the person is aloof, distant, or uncommunicative.

One symptom of burnout is striking out in anger or with hostility. Another is being alienated and depressed. Emotional exhaustion is feeling drained or used up. Once emotional exhaustion sets in, a person feels unable to give to others and may respond by cutting off involvement with others or pushing them away with anger or hostility.

Burnout is created from environments where other people are angry, cynical, or emotional or where there is frustration, crises, or pain. These environments provide little support or positive feedback, where people hear little praise when things go well but constant criticism when something goes wrong. Some environments put people in constant touch with others who are upsetting, depressing, or disagreeable.

Emotionally or physically overloading environments challenge a person's ability to cope as well. In these situations, there are too many demands for the person to do a competent job. The immediate reaction to an overloaded situation is to provide a quicker and more impersonal response. The job is still completed, but with emotional detachment. Eventually an overloading environment leads to burnout.

These conditions are precursors to burnout.

❖ Unrealistically high expectations for oneself
❖ Unrealistically high expectations of what the world should be like
❖ A sense of powerlessness in being able to remedy problems in the workplace
❖ Experiencing a lack of support or encouragement from supervisors
❖ Preoccupation with work and putting in long hours to the exclusion of outside activities.

Check the list below and see if any of these symptoms apply to you. If you checked more than four items, corrective action is vital.

❑ Working long hours with the assumption that more time on the job will ease the stress
❑ Exhaustion/fatigue- constantly feeling tired and lack of energy

- ❑ Dreading going to work each day
- ❑ Feeling powerless over decisions made at work
- ❑ Unclear about job responsibilities
- ❑ Feel that everything you do requires an 'effort'
- ❑ Lack of understanding about the purpose of work
- ❑ Feeling caught in the middle
- ❑ Work is not challenging and/or too little to do
- ❑ Being overqualified for the work done
- ❑ Unclear expectations
- ❑ Consistent lack of feedback from supervisors
- ❑ Job completed is unappreciated
- ❑ Unclear of the 'rules' and/or priorities
- ❑ Work is unrewarding or unsatisfying
- ❑ Not respected by those you work with
- ❑ Lack of career direction
- ❑ No hope for advancement or growth in current position
- ❑ Not believing in the company and/or job values
- ❑ Loss or increase of appetite
- ❑ Frequent illness
- ❑ Constant muscle tension
- ❑ Bored and detached from work and home activities and people
- ❑ Impatient and irritable with people at work and at home
- ❑ Inability to concentrate and a decreasing quality of work
- ❑ Negative, cynical and hostile attitudes toward others, particularly superiors
- ❑ Loss of self-esteem and self-confidence
- ❑ Blaming someone else when things go wrong
- ❑ Feeling stuck because of financial obligations, the location, or the threat of unemployment

It is not difficult to see that stress affects the brain in many ways. Think about it in your daily life. Does added stress help you think through problems? Or when under stress do you need a little quiet time to reflect? Those under a great deal of stress often have trouble thinking clearly and making good decisions. These affects also translate into problems for the body when the brain cannot properly rest because of anxiety and stress.

What is stress doing to your body?

What happens to your body when you are stressed is because the fight or flight response automatically kicks in. This is great when you need to run out of the way of an oncoming car. It's a problem when there is no need to run yet the body is primed to do so. This is why we end up with stress-related issues.

When you are under stress, your hormones kick in and make changes in your body. Your heart speeds up, the blood flow to your brain slows down and the blood flow to your muscles speed up (up to 400%!). Your digestion stops so it doesn't take energy from the muscles and your muscle tension increases. You breathe faster to bring more oxygen to your muscles. You are ready to run or fight! If there is no ensuing fight, your body doesn't know what to do with all the ready-for-action steps it has taken.

Clearly your body is ready to do something but there is nothing to do. That is how the body responds each and every time you feel stressed. Can you imagine how having this happen over and over again can seriously affect your health?

Stress can affect all aspects of your physical body, including:

❖ Sexual desire
❖ Menopause or PMS symptoms

❖ Erectile dysfunction
❖ How you process your food and what nutrients are absorbed
❖ Your appetite (either more or less thus your weight)
❖ Your blood sugar level/Diabetes

It's important that you pay attention to your body so you can be aware of any physical changes that may be a sign that you are under stress. The physical symptoms of stress vary by person but can include any of the following:

❖ Headache
❖ Insomnia
❖ Hot or cold flashes
❖ Dry mouth and/or difficulty swallowing
❖ A pounding heart and/or rapid heartbeat
❖ Difficulty breathing
❖ Stomach upset
❖ Frequent urination or diarrhea
❖ Sweaty palms
❖ Tight muscles
❖ Dizziness
❖ Fatigue

Any changes in your physical health can be a sign that you are under stress. Sometimes we ignore the signs our body gives us because we are busy focusing on what's going on around us. If you have any physical symptoms of pain or any of the symptoms listed above, it is important to stop and check in with yourself. This is the time to do a stress reducing practice like the ones in Part 3 of this book.

STRESS CURVE

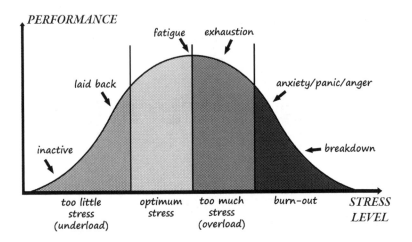

The Stress Curve shows how you can go from no stress as at all to burn-out. Notice that it also shows that an optimum level of stress is good. It's a balancing act to have just the right amount of stress; too much stress or too little stress is equally problematic.

The infographic below shows the effects of stress on your body:

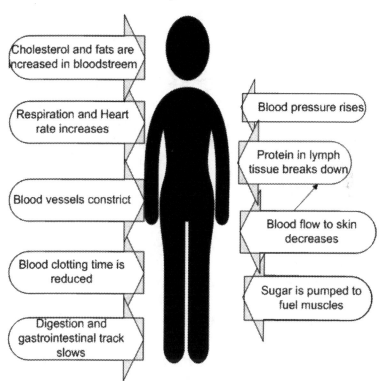

What is stress doing to your spirit?

Many self-help authors say that spirituality is the true key to changing both your subconscious and thus your thoughts. They believe that only through a spiritually-based belief system will people be able to heal past wounds and change painful thought patterns. If you believe that there is a higher power at work in your life you will feel less turmoil when confronted with the stressors of daily life. Carl Jung believed that each person is longing to reunite with the Source, and that it was a major contributor to the effectiveness of psychotherapy. Whether they are Eastern or Western in origin, spiritual beliefs can change thoughts for the better.

Stress affects your spirit in immeasurable ways. If you are stressed, there is less chance that you will take the time to honor your spirit and do whatever spiritual practices you would normally do.

What is spirit? I cannot define spirit for you because spirit is a personal thing. However, I can say that I believe that it is something bigger than me; something that I can't see or touch but still exists. We are all aware of our body and our mind. For me, spirit is something that is 'bigger' than me. Spirit has many 'names'. For some it is God, Abba, Holy Spirit, Buddha, The Universe, Source, Higher Self, and so on.

You probably didn't think about Spirit being affected by stress, but it is. When you are stressed, you are less likely to take the time to recognize Spirit and its importance in your life. Spirit is that which lifts you up when you're down. Spirit is what gives meaning to your life. Spirit is the big picture. When we say "everything happens for a reason" we are referring to Spirit.

Spiritual practices are easy to forget about when you are feeling stressed. It's difficult to even think sometimes when you are stressed, much less consider anything spiritual. However, this is the most important time to reconnect with Spirit. Whatever your definition of Spirit is, you need to remember to honor it and spend time with it, especially when you are under stress.

Spirit can bring you to a place of acceptance and peace when you are feeling stressed. Spirit can remind you that "this too shall pass." Spirit can help you slow down and take a look at what is causing your stress and how you can lessen it.

If you pray, pray for clarity and understanding. Ask Spirit to help you slow down and show you the way to get back on track. With Spirit's help you will feel better immediately. You will understand that what is stressing you is probably not all that important after all. And if it is important, you will know that not only will it pass, but that you can handle it in a positive and loving way. Spirit supports you and helps you understand that things happen but that what really matters is Love.

PART 2

THE TESTS

Finding your astrological sign

It may be general but there are definitely commonalities for all Aries, Capricorns, etc. Each astrological sign does, indeed, describe to some degree what stress-relieving practices that may work for you. Using your astrological sign can also give you a quick reference on where to start. It's easy and often a great place to start.

Read the information for your sign below. This is your birth sign, based on when you were born, and is what you see in the newspapers and other astrological predictions. However, the birth sign is very general. If for whatever reason, you do not agree with the information below for your birth sign then choose one you do agree with.

There are often other aspects to your full astrological chart that influence you more than your Sun sign. While the Sun sign, also known as the birth sign, can give you a very general idea of your personality, a full birth chart is much more specific. The Sun sign is the one that most folks look to but there are other parts to astrology that define more of who you are. An astrological birth chart is laid out like a pie chart. Each piece of the pie is a different part of your life – home, money, work, etc. Within this chart are placed the planets that affect that part of your life. Together, this creates a more detailed description of your personality than just your Sun sign. My birth chart is shown below so you can see what one looks like.

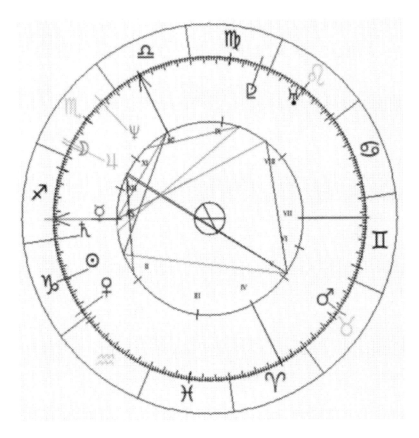

There are numerous websites where you can get your chart done. You will need the time and place of your birth. Most online astrological birth charts include a general description of the various planets and houses and what they mean in your chart. It can be eye-opening and validating at the same time. However, you don't need your birth chart to determine which of the signs you feel describes you best. Just read all the listings, if you want, and see which feels most right for you.

Additionally, the Sun sign that you know may be affected by the sign just before or after it if you were born at a time that is within three days before or after the starting or ending date of your sign. This is called the cusp. For example, Michael was born on September 23rd, so he will have aspects of Virgo and Libra. In that case, he would look at both and decide which one is most like him.

This list of the astrological dates and times includes some key words for each sign and a short statement about how the sign affects what practices may be applicable.

March 21 to April 20
Aries – spontaneous – active - independent
Aries will start new practice enthusiastically but then dwindle out in a fairly short period of time. They need a variety of practices to choose from that are active and that they can do whenever they want to.

April 21 to May 20, 21
Taurus – practical – pleasure-oriented – grounded
As long as the practice provides a sense of comfort and regularity Taurus will be fine with the same practice for a long period of time.

May 21 to June 21
Gemini – very active – nimble – variety
Gemini needs a variety of practices to choose from. Gemini's are mentally quick and fond of questioning. Their practice needs to make sense to them and the practice itself needs to be 'distracting' from their ever-working mind for them in some way.

June 22 to July 22

Cancer – intuitive – gentle – comforting

Cancers need a practice where they feel comfortable and comforted. They will not do well with anything that involves loud or boisterous sounds or activities.

July 23 to August 22

Leo – expressive – creative – dramatic

Leos need a practice that provides them with a bit of drama and allows them to express themselves. They prefer a practice that provides them with a sense of self-mastery.

August 23 to September 22

Virgo- analytical – task-oriented – systemized practice

Virgos need a practice that has a specific systemization to it. They will most likely prefer it be done at the same time each day at the same time; preferably it is simple and short.

September 23 to October 22

Libra – options-oriented – cooperative – esthetics

Libras will prefer to have a variety of practices which they feel are esthetically pleasing as well as healing. They will generally do well in a group setting. An introverted Libra will be fine alone but will still prefer to have a practice that varies and that they feel is esthetically pleasing.

October 23 to November 22

Scorpio – transforming – intense – ritual

Scorpios will prefer a practice that includes an aspect of ritual to it. They will do well with individual or group practice as long as it is not foo-foo. Scorpios need a bit of intensity in their practice.

November 23 to December 21
Sagittarius – questioning – individual – philosophical
Sagittarians need a practice that provides them with things to think about and question. Their practice must include some elements of philosophy and discussion, whether it comes from working in a group and then discussing the practice after it is over or working alone and then discussing things with friends or family.

December 22 to January 20
Capricorn – organization – strong – pragmatic
Capricorns need a practice where they feel that there is an end in sight. They need to know where the practice is going and how long it will be before they get there. They will generally be fine with a daily practice that allows them to make step-by-step progress in their practice.

January 21 to February 19
Aquarius – innovative – spurts of energy – nontraditional
Aquarians need a practice that provides them with the feeling of being inventive. They will most likely pull from a variety of practices and put them together for themselves.

February 20 to March 20
Pisces – escapist –rhythmic– all spiritual
Pisces will prefer a practice that allows them to feel that they are in a different reality or in a different place. This could be by way of drumming or some other rhythmic movements or by listening to a guided meditation.

Finding your Mind, Body, Spirit type

This test will help you determine if you want to focus on mind, body, or spirit practices. The test will show you where you are most comfortable. However, you could choose to pick an area that you are not comfortable with and learn some new skills. For example, if you find that you are body-focused, and not very spiritual-focused, you could do mostly body practices and add a few spiritual practices to build up that area of your life.

Answer each question by ranking each statement as common, less common and least common for you.

1 = Most common for me
2 = Less common for me
3 = Least common for me

Try to go with the first intuitive feeling you get; don't think about it too much – just number 1, 2 or 3 for each statement and then move on to the next question.

1. When I make a decision, I usually base it on:
_____ A. Fact
_____ B. Practicality
_____ C. Values

2. When someone tells me that I did I good job, I like it to be based on:

_____ A. An idea I came up with

_____ B. Completing a project

_____ C. How I helped others

3. If I could be considered special in any area of my life, I would want it to be:

_____ A. My intelligence

_____ B. My health and fitness

_____ C. How I make others feel good about themselves

4. If I had to describe my ideal day at home it would involve:

_____ A. Reading, "surfing the net", learning something

_____ B. Exercise, working in the yard, building something

_____ C. Something spiritual

5. If you asked someone what I go overboard on, they would probably say:

_____ A. I think too much

_____ B. I can't sit still; I seem to have to move around a lot

_____ C. I am preoccupied with how to help others

6. The word that my friends and family would say describe me best is:

_____ A. Intellectual

_____ B. Active

_____ C. Deeply feeling

7. When I describe experiences that I've had, I tend to remember:

_____ A. How the events happened and why

_____ B. What I did

_____ C. What the experience meant to me

8. To me, a good experience is one that:

_____ A. Teaches me something

_____ B. Gets me in touch with my body

_____ C. Helps me feel connected to something greater than myself

Count up all the scores by adding all the A. Answers, B Answers, and C. Answers

Total of all A answers:_____

Total of all B answers:_____

Total of all C answers:_____

If your A's are **lowest** that means you tend toward Mind practices

If your B's are **lowest** that means you tend to prefer Body practices

If your C's are the **lowest** that means you tend to prefer Spirit practices

The Chart

Below is the list of suggested practices for each astrological sign and by Mind, Body, and Spirit practices. **This chart will help you get started finding the practices for you but feel free to try other practices that interest you!**

To read the chart:

1. Find your astrological sign in the first column.
2. Find your preferred modality (Mind, Body or Spirit) in the columns.
3. Locate your suggested practices in the Practices section of the book.
   For example, Aires with Mind preference would go to the Mind section and find
   Mind-11, Mind-17, Mind-21, and Mind-21. The numbers are found in the left side of the practice box.

	Mind	Body	Spirit
Aries	10	7	2
	11	11	7
	14	15	10
	17	20	17
	21	21	19

Taurus	3 4 8 12 19	1 6 8 14 18	6 7 10 17 19
Gemini	2 5 13 15 20	7 4 14 19 23	3 6 12 14 17
Cancer	3 7 11 12 21	2 6 10 15 18	3 7 10 18 20
Leo	4 6 7 11 19	3 7 16 19 22	5 6 10 14 17
Virgo	1 6 9 10 14	1 5 8 14 21	2 5 8 12 16
Libra	1 13 14 15 18	3 4 10 12 19	4 7 13 16 19

Scorpio	2 8 10 12 19	6 9 14 17 20	1 6 11 16 18
Sagittarius	3 5 16 18 20	5 10 18 19 22	1 2 3 17 18
Capricorn	2 8 10 12 15	2 10 11 14 18	5 6 11 17 19
Aquarius	4 11 14 18 21	3 7 16 19 21	3 8 12 18 20
Pisces	6 8 11 12 17	4 11 14 18 19	2 5 10 14 19

PART 3

THE PRACTICES

The lists below are broken into Mind, Body, and Spirit. In some cases, it was very difficult to choose just one modality and some could argue successfully that the practice is a different modality than the one I have put it in. I chose the modality based on which one was most appropriate.

Please keep in mind that what you do to your mind affects your body and spirit, and what you do to your body affects your mind and spirit. They all work together in one way or another. Therefore, while a practice may be mostly a single modality, it **is** affecting the rest of you as well. And that is a very good thing!

Each practice includes the modality, a suggested time frame for practicing, and a step-by-step guide on how to do the practice. All Mind practices are together, as are all Body practices and all Spirit practices are together.

A bit about meditation

Meditation can be extremely helpful for relieving stress. In the past three decades, there has been a lot of research with meditation and what it can do for you. Studies have shown regular Meditation practice can produce measurable effects that are the opposite of the fight or flight stress response. Other physiological effects of meditation include:

- ❖ Improved mental and emotional health
- ❖ Reduced perception of stress
- ❖ Reduced anxiety and depression
- ❖ Increased degree of self-actualization
- ❖ Increased locus of control (feeling in control of your life circumstances)
- ❖ Improved sleep
- ❖ Decreased tendency to worry
- ❖ Improved concentration and focus
- ❖ Enhanced feelings of happiness
- ❖ Increased sense of peace and well-being
- ❖ Increased awareness and spiritual calm
- ❖ Decreased fear
- ❖ Increased mindfulness
- ❖ Decreased psychological "rumination" (going over and over the same thing)
- ❖ Increased ability to regulate behavior
- ❖ Increased resilience and adaptability

You probably already knew that meditation is very, very good for you. The point here is that there are a number of meditations in the practices. Please consider giving them a try. If you find a meditation that you enjoy and can continue for a period of time, you will have a lot less stress. The key is to have a regular practice for 20 minutes one or two times every day. The majority of the studies that show significant gain from meditation include people who do the meditation for 20 minutes every day for a year or more. However, if you cannot commit to that much time, do the best you can. I have been meditating on and off for almost 40 years. What I have found for myself is that I do best with a body-based practice. Maybe that is all you need to find as well. Either way please consider a meditation practice of some sort on a regular basis to reduce your stress.

Effects of Meditation on Specific Health Conditions

Meditation is beneficial for those with medical conditions, especially conditions caused by stress. Research has shown meditation to be helpful for the conditions listed below.

Condition	Meditation helps with:	Suggested Mediation type
Anxiety	Worrying; Shortness of breath; Increased heart rate	Any
Chronic Pain	Perception of pain; blood pressure; anxiety associated with chronic pain	Mindfulness
Depression		Mindfulness; Transcendental Meditation
Hypertension	Blood pressure	Transcendental Meditation
Coronary Artery Disease (CAD)	Hypertension; atherosclerosis	Transcendental Meditation

Cancer	Related symptoms such as anxiety, depression, pain, fatigue, sleep disturbances	Any
Substance Abuse	Prevention/recovery	Mindfulness; Transcendental Meditation

Contraindications for Meditation

Meditation is considered safe for most all people. However, some reports have shown that psychotic disorders and those with other serious mental conditions should consult their doctors prior to doing meditation on their own. It is also not advisable to use meditation as the sole treatment for any serious illness. Meditation is meant as an adjunct to any medical treatments for those with serious illnesses.

Guidelines for Practicing Meditation

❖ Beginning a meditation practice is a beneficial way to increase or enhance your current health or support your other modalities.

❖ Meditate on an empty stomach to avoid feeling drowsy or falling asleep.

❖ Start with shorter sessions (such as 5 minutes twice a day instead of 20 minutes or longer once a day) until you feel comfortable with your practice.

❖ Practice regular, daily meditation. Don't give up if it seems challenging. Keep up your practice!

❖ Choose a method of meditation that fits with your intuition, needs, beliefs, etc. Experiment with several different types.

❖ There is no "right" way to meditate.

❖ Everyone will experience the "monkey mind' and will need to gently refocus when the mind wanders.

Quick Overview of Types of Meditation

The various types of meditation may include specific features such as focused attention, relaxed breathing, a quiet setting, prayer, reflection, and focused attention on a sacred object or being. There's no right way or wrong way to meditate. It can be done by anyone, of any age, in any location.

- ❖ Deep Breathing – Focusing on the breath, the practitioner inhales and exhales slowly and deeply. This practice is often added to other practices such as those listed below.
- ❖ Body Focus – Intense focus on different parts of the body allows the practitioner to experience the pain, tension, warmth or relaxation of the body
- ❖ Walking – Usually walking at a fairly slow pace, the practitioner focuses on the movement of the legs or feet while often repeating words in his/her mind such as "placing" as each foot is raised and placed on the ground
- ❖ Mindfulness – Originally rooted in Eastern meditation practices, Mindfulness is now used in a variety of healthcare settings. Mindfulness is about being aware of whatever is happening in the current moment by focusing on awareness of the breath, body, mind, and environment. The most common mindfulness meditation approach used in health care settings is the secular Mindfulness Based Stress Reduction (MBSR) approach developed by Kabat-Zinn at the University of Massachusetts in the late 1970s.
- ❖ Centering Prayer – This method comes from the Christian contemplative tradition. The goal is to establish a deep and personal connection with God through silence and stillness. Each thought that comes to mind is released as the goal is letting go of

the power of thought so the practitioner is open to guidance from God.

❖ Transcendental Meditation ™ (TM) – In this practice, the practitioner sits silently with eyes closed in a state of restful alertness. The practitioner repeats a mantra (See Body-20) silently in his/her mind. Meditators usually practice TM for 20 minutes in the morning and 20 minutes in the evening.

Mind practices

Mind-1 ♦ Breathing Break

Suggested time of practice: Three minutes

How to do it:

1. Stop what you are doing and...
2. Take a deep breath in, counting to 8
3. Hold the breath for the count of 8
4. Let the breath out to the count of 8

Repeat until the 3 minutes are up.

Mind-2 ♦ Self Talk

Suggested time of practice: Hourly

How to do it:

Be aware of your self-talk!

❖ The messages you send to yourself through your own internal self-talk are essential to how you view yourself.

Since how you view yourself is an important aspect of stress, these messages are the ones you should explore on a regular basis. Your self-talk affects your self-esteem, so if you have 'issues' with your self-esteem (and don't we all to one degree or another?) consider exploring this area more fully.

❖ To become aware of your self-talk, try setting an hourly alarm. When the alarm goes off, stop and think back to what you've been telling yourself for the past hour.

❖ You may want to journal or make notes on negative self-talk and write a positive self-talk statement at the same time.

❖ You can keep this positive self-talk statement on a piece of paper that you refer to when you notice yourself engaging in negative self-talk.

Mind-3 ♦ Stress Journal

Suggested time of practice: Daily or As Needed

<u>How to do it</u>:

Below is a sample of what you should include in your Stress Journal. Please refer to the section *What is Stress doing to your mind?* For information about the *From Problem to Project* section below.

Date _____

Time _____

Stressor _____

Thought _____

Physical Reaction _____

Thought or belief / Habit / Environment / History

(Turn around the action/ thought/ outcome)

_____

_____

_____

From Problem to Project

_____

_____

_____

Here is an example:

6/25/XX

12:45 PM

Late getting back to work from lunch

Boss is going to be angry

Stomach feeling queasy

Environment – the boss IS angry when I get back late from lunch so I should go to boss and apologize as soon as I get in (this usually appeases her).

P to P: I hate feeling this way and I hate that my boss treats me like a child. I will work towards either creating a more mature relationship with her, or start looking for a better job. Since work is hard to find right now, I'll first try to create a more mature relationship. First I need to determine how to do that. I'll ask my friend Gloria about it since she has been a boss for a while. I'll also check out the library for books that may help. Then...

Mind-4 ♦ Check Your Self Talk

Suggested time of practice: None

<u>How to do it:</u>

Albert Ellis (a psychologist who developed Rational Emotive Behavior Therapy) developed an approach to help people replace irrational beliefs with realistic statements. He called this approach *Cognitive Restructuring*. He suggested that a person's thoughts are what create anger, anxiety, and hostility. Although his model looks simple, it is a very powerful and helpful way to lessen stress in your life.

A------------------------------B------------------------------C

For every (A) activating event, there is a (B) belief (automatic thought that we tell ourselves about the event). The emotional and physical consequences of the belief about the event are the consequence (C). Most people think that A causes C. In reality, it is B, our self-talk, that has the greater influence.

When an upsetting event occurs, our automatic thoughts run through our minds. Because an upsetting event happens so quickly, we usually don't have time to stop and think about the thoughts that run through our heads. If the automatic thoughts are distorted, we are more likely to react negatively to the situation. If we spend time between events examining our self-talk, we can 're-program' distorted automatic thoughts to be more realistic.

Important Note:
Distorted automatic thought patterns are learned throughout our lives, often in childhood. Therefore, our history plays a major part in the programming of distorted automatic thoughts. If you feel uncomfortable challenging your distorted automatic thoughts on your own you should seek the assistance of a trained professional. Psychologists and psychiatrists are trained to work with people that have distorted automatic thought patterns.

When you feel depressed or angry, ask yourself, "What is my self-talk?" This self-talk, and not the event is what produces the emotions you feel. To assess your self-talk, ask yourself the following questions:

1. Is there any rational support for the thought?
2. What evidence exists for the incorrectness of the thought?
3. What evidence exists for the correctness of the thought?
4. What is the worst thing that might happen to me? Is this really so bad?

5. What good things might possibly occur if the worst case actually happens?

Fighting angry or depressing emotions takes a commitment to ask yourself the above questions whenever a strong emotions arises.

After you've determined your automatic thought patterns (that's the hard part), you can work to replace them with more realistic and positive thoughts. For example, if your automatic thought is that you have to be on time for everything, you can rewrite the thought as "I am usually on time."

The most common distorted automatic thought patterns are listed below. Being aware of these will help you in determining your own distorted thoughts.

❖ Focusing on the negative, even if the situation is mostly positive
❖ Assuming that you know what someone else is thinking
❖ Exaggerating the negative in a situation
❖ Pessimistically predicting a negative outcome without testing the evidence
❖ Assuming that the worst thing possible will always happen
❖ Thinking in extremes and black-and-white (either I'm ____ or ____ but never in between)
❖ Making rigid demands of ourselves or others (using shoulds/musts/oughts)
❖ Thinking that your feelings are always an accurate representation of reality (Remember, your feelings are the result of your thinking!)
❖ Overgeneralizing

❖ Personalizing (seeing yourself as more responsible than you are)
❖ Blaming
❖ Making unfavorable comparisons
❖ Regretting decisions, actions, etc. from the past

Whenever you come across one of these distorted automatic thought patterns, make your statement ("I know what he's thinking!") and then turn it around ("I can't read his mind, I will ask him what he's thinking."). If this doesn't work, go over the questions previously mentioned until you can rewrite the thought so it's realistic. Here are some to try:

1. He's going to get fired for that!
2. I am a bad person for saying what I did!
3. If I obtain perfection nothing bad will ever happen to me again!
4. He treated me so miserably. He has ruined my life and my self-esteem!
5. Brian is such a great guy. Look at all he does for the community! I could never do as much as he does.

--◦◦-- ---••◦◦••◦◦-- --◦◦---

Mind-5 ♦ Subconscious Self-programing

Suggested time of practice: As Needed

<u>How to do it:</u>

Studies have shown that the *most effective and long-lasting benefits* come from changing the *subconscious*. How do we do that? Basically, there are 5 "Gateways to the Subconscious" - in other words, 5 ways to change subconscious thoughts. Keep in mind, however, that any thought patterns that exist must be replaced, not simply erased. Psychology has shown that trying to remove a habit or thought without replacing it with something else is rarely, if ever, effective.

The "Gateways to the Subconscious," in order from the amount of time it takes for them to change the subconscious are:

1. Repetition - this takes the most time but can work (hence the effectiveness of affirmations!)
2. An authority figure- this gateway is most 'open' when we are younger. As we age we are less vulnerable to new subconscious programming by authority figures. Additionally, we have a stronger tendency to rebel against authority figures as we age. Generally, we will respond to authority figures with either "obey" or "rebel".
3. Desire for Identity- whether we like it or not, we have an ego that craves belonging, acceptance, recognition, and love. This can take the form of accepting Peer Pressure and going along with whatever is proposed so as to be part of the group. A mentor can also be a strong subconscious programmer if we feel strongly that we want to 'be like him or her." Keep in mind that all desires for recognition, acceptance, and love can program your subconscious either negatively or positively. It is up to the individual to determine which it is. Ultimately, if we can reward, accept, and love ourselves we are much less likely to be 'programmed' by another.
4. Hypnosis - when your mind enters the alpha state, the subconscious becomes receptive to new programming. We'll talk a bit more about this below.

5. Strong emotions at the time of the thought- this is the most powerful way possible to impact the subconscious. One minute of intense emotion can permanently impact the subconscious. Whenever we enter an emotional state of mind, we become vulnerable to subconscious programming. Furthermore, as the emotions intensify, the emotional energy drives the imprinting deeper into the subconscious. We must monitor our thoughts when we experience any kind of emotion where the emotion is positive OR negative. When you rehearse certain words or actions mentally while experiencing emotion, your subconscious records these impressions. This rehearsal creates the potential for imagined words or actions to come out automatically. Therefore, emotion makes us even more vulnerable to suggestion than does hypnosis, so it behooves each of us to learn what to do when our buttons get pushed. The good news is that using emotions while under hypnosis is the quickest way to change the subconscious. A hypnotist can be essential in helping you with this practice.

Mind-6 ✦ Getting Real

Suggested time of practice: As Needed

<u>How to do it:</u>

Be realistic about what you have control over!

Feeling that everything in your life is in your control prompts unnecessary stress. The truth is - you only have control over yourself and your reactions to what happens to you. Far too many people feel that they can control others with the way they act. Certainly there is an amount of truth in this, as how we respond to someone does affect his or her response back. However, they are a complex being just as you are and you cannot know exactly what their motivations, desires, and secrets are. Be realistic when dealing with others. You cannot control them. You can ask them for what you need and ask that they follow through, but you cannot MAKE them do anything, just as no one else can MAKE YOU do something (unless they are threatening you and at that point you need the police, not a stress relief book).

Mind-7 ♦ Pretend

Suggested time of practice: As Needed

<u>How to do it:</u>

If you feel that you are definitely a Type A (overachiever, time urgency, etc.) and want to change, begin by pretending to be calm, non-competitive, and patient. This can work for any personality change you want to make - just pretend and before you know it you won't be 'pretending' anymore! And, please, no guilt over being Type A – it's not a personality disorder. It's more like a socially acceptable obsession!

Mind-8 ✦ STOP!

Suggested time of practice: As Needed

How to do it:

Try thought-stopping:

When you have a thought that is creating stress for you, simply tell yourself "STOP". By repeating this every time you have a stressful thought, you can reduce or eliminate the thought.

Mind-9 ✦ Be Imperfect

Suggested time of practice: As Needed

How to do it:

The belief that you must be perfect or do something perfectly usually comes from a feeling of inadequacy. Working in this area can be difficult and long lasting or, simple and quick. When you realize that it is humanly impossible to be perfect and accept the truth of this statement, then you can be free from the need to do anything perfect. Simply remind yourself "I do the best I can and it is good enough."

As for failing or making a mistake (which is only human), I think Ben Franklin said it best: "I have not failed, I've found 10,000 ways that don't work."

Mind-10 ✦ Laughing Meditation

Suggested time of practice: 3-20 minutes

How to do it:

Did you know that although children laugh about 400 times a day, adults laugh only about 15 times per day—the same number of times they get angry?

Laughing:

- ❖ Lowers blood pressure
- ❖ Reduces stress hormone levels, especially epinephrine and cortisol
- ❖ Increases immunoglobulin A antibodies and improves the immune system
- ❖ Dilates the endothelium (the inner lining of blood vessels) and increases blood flow throughout the body
- ❖ Increases lung capacity and the availability of oxygen for the body
- ❖ Increases endorphin levels in the body (the body's natural painkillers)
- ❖ Reduces symptoms of pain in individuals with arthritis and migraine headaches
- ❖ Stimulates the uptake of dopamine (the "feel good" neurotransmitter)

Lighten up- if you think, "someday you'll look back on this and laugh"- why not laugh now? Laughing actually stimulates the production and release of healthy chemicals in the body!

Laughter meditation can be practiced alone or in a group. You can watch or listen to a recording or video of laughter meditation at any time of the day or night. Here are some guidelines for practicing laughter meditation:

- Every morning upon awakening, do some stretches. Stretch like babies do when they wake up after sleeping. Feel every muscle being stretched.
- Without opening your eyes, begin to laugh. At first it will take some effort but soon real laughter will begin to rise up within you. Once the laughter takes over, just let it happen.
- There is no recommended duration, so laugh until you are tired of laughing. You will be able to sustain the laugher for longer and longer periods of time.

Practiced in the evening, laughter meditation is a powerful relaxant.

Mind-11 ♦ Manage Your Time

Suggested time of practice: As Needed

How to do it:

If you are not sure what you Want to do as compared to what you Need to do, consider using the chart below.

1. Fold a piece of paper in half. Then fold it again so you have 4 squares.
2. On the top, write Have To in the first box and Don't Have To in the second box.
3. Along the left side, write Want to in the first box and Don't Want to in the bottom box.

4. Write down all the tasks you have to compete. Then fill in the grid by sorting each task into one of the four boxes. Anything that falls into the Don't Want To/ Don't Have To box you can feel free to stop doing!

With practice you'll be able to visualize what belongs in that category automatically.

	Have to do	Don't Have To
Want To Do		
Don't Want To Do		

Mind-12 ♦ Liming

Suggested time of practice: Daily or As Needed

<u>How to do it:</u>

Liming is the Caribbean art of doing nothing, guilt-free, a revitalizing habit that's virtually unheard of in United States. Liming can free you from the Type A desire to fill every waking minute with 'something productive'.

The basic idea of liming is to shift yourself out of the rat race – as completely and deeply as you can – for at least ten minutes a day. You can use those ten minutes in any way you want, such as

- ❖ Meditation
- ❖ Listening to escape music (whatever that may be is up to you)
- ❖ Leaning back in your chair and looking out the window
- ❖ Reading an upbeat book
- ❖ Remembering a favorite vacation

Mind-13 ♦ Yes and No

Suggested time of practice: 5 minutes

<u>How to do it:</u>

This practice is both a physical and a mind practice. You will need a friend who is willing to help you (it will help them, too!) OR you can do this in a mirror.

1. Stand facing your partner.

2. One of you will say "NO!"
3. The other will say "YES!"
4. Repeat this going back and forth using all the gestures that you use when you are adamant about something.
5. Do this for 2 minutes and then switch roles.

After both of you have had the chance to do both YES! and NO! discuss what it felt like. Hint: If it's hard for you to say NO! then you just practiced it with conviction. That may have been difficult but saying NO! is important part of reducing stress!

Mind-14 ♦ Daydream

Suggested time of practice: 20 Minutes

How to do it:

Daydreaming is also recommended in the Body practices with rocking (See Body 18) included because daydreaming is so powerful. Studies have shown that daydreaming has the same brain wave patterns as those induced when meditating. Try to simply follow whatever comes to you in your mind. Try not to focus but just let the thoughts come and go as they will.

Mind-15 ♦ Transcendental Meditation

Suggested time of practice: 20 minutes

How to do it:

Transcendental Meditation techniques allow the mind to progressively experience higher levels of thought until the mind is in a state of restful alertness. Once in this state, the body is able to relax and rejuvenate. Meditators usually practice 20 minutes in the morning and 20 minutes in the evening.

To practice Transcendental Meditation, follow these guidelines.

❖ Choose a mantra (See Body-20) (a sound, syllable, word, or phrase on which to focus).

❖ Choose a quiet, comfortable place and lie or sit down.

❖ Close the eyes and relax each part of the body, starting with the feet and working to the top of the head.

❖ Consciously breathe slower and slower to deepen the state of relaxation.

❖ Focus and repeat the mantra softly for about a minute. Repeat the mantra more softly each time.

❖ Focus on feeling a connection to life itself, while repeating the mantra for about 20 minutes. When distracting thoughts appear, allow them to drift away. Return the focus to the mantra.

Mind-16 ♦ Mindfulness Meditation

Suggested time of practice: 20 minutes

How to do it:

Mindfulness mediation is so simple that it actually seems difficult. It involves focusing on only your breath and nothing else. The practice of mindfulness meditation includes seven key factors:

- ❖ **Non-judging** involves the meditator releasing the need to judge or change the thoughts, sounds, objects, or emotions that occur during meditation. Non-judging means seeing and accepting things as they are, and simply recognizing judgments.
- ❖ **Patience** involves practicing patience. Meditators remain in the present moment because they are not thinking about the future or the past. Patience with their abilities to meditate effectively is also important.
- ❖ **Beginner's mind** expresses the ability to be open, eager, accepting, and have no preconceptions about what occurs during meditation. In the beginner's mind there are many possibilities, while in the expert's mind there are few.
- ❖ **Trust** involves having faith in the process and being open to the meditation experience, trusting in what is revealed, and trusting our intuition, awareness, and experience.
- ❖ **Non-striving** involves the ability to just be, know that there is nowhere to go, nothing to do at this moment, and nothing to attain. This factor is also called "being in the now."

❖ **Acceptance** means letting go of the need to have things manifest in the way we want them to manifest and, instead, allowing them to unfold. It also involves acknowledging things as they are "in the present moment."

❖ **Letting go** is similar to the concept of non-attachment. In particular, it means letting go of the past and the expectations of the future and having faith in the process of meditation without any attachment to the outcomes.

To practice mindfulness meditation, follow these guidelines:

1. Find a comfortable posture that embodies wakefulness (such as sitting on a cushion or comfortable chair, walking, standing, or lying down).
2. Choose a time of day when you are fairly awake. If you are alert, you might want to close your eyes. If you are drowsy or tired, you might want to keep your eyes open.
3. Choose a time to meditate during which you will not be interrupted. Turn off all electronic devices.
4. Begin by taking two or three deep breaths.
5. Let go of thoughts of the past and future, and allow your body and mind to relax.
6. Breathe normally during the meditation.
7. Do not focus on anything specific but instead be fully aware of and alert to what is going on in the present moment.
8. If thoughts, sounds, feelings, or physical sensations enter your awareness, gently bring your attention back to your breathing.
9. Sit quietly for 10 to 20 minutes and observe your breath.

Mindfulness can be cultivated during any activity, including sitting, standing, walking, eating, and even while taking a shower, cooking, exercising, or sharing intimate moments with loved ones.

See also the Chocolate Mindfulness Meditation (Mind-17)

Mind-17 ♦ Chocolate Mindfulness Meditation

Suggested time of practice: 20 minutes

<u>How to do it:</u>

The chocolate meditation is one of the most pleasurable forms of mindfulness meditation. Choose a piece of chocolate (preferably dark) that you have never tried before or one that you haven't eaten recently. Allow at least 15 to 20 minutes for this meditation.

1. Take a few deep breaths to relax your body.
2. Open the wrapper. Inhale the aroma. Let it sweep over you.
3. Break off a piece and look at it. Let your eyes take in what it looks like, examining every part of it.
4. Place it in your mouth. See if it's possible to hold it on your tongue and let it melt, experiencing the sensations in your mouth. Chocolate has over 300 different flavors. See if you can sense some of them.
5. If other thoughts come into your mind during the meditation, gently refocus your attention back to the present moment.

6. Once the chocolate has completely melted, swallow it very slowly and deliberately. Allow it to trickle down your throat.
7. Repeat this procedure with the next piece.
8. Write down how you felt. Was it different than normal? Did the chocolate taste better than it would have if you had eaten it in your normal way?

Mind-18 ♦ Vipassana Meditation

Suggested time of practice: 20 minutes

<u>How to do it:</u>

Vipassana meditation focuses on the deep interconnection between the mind and body. From the time of Buddha to the present day, Vipassana has been passed down by an unbroken chain of teachers.

Practitioners begin this meditation by observing the natural breath as a way to focus the mind. With a sharpened awareness, they proceed to observe the changing nature of body and mind, and experience the universal truths of impermanence, suffering, and egolessness. The entire path focuses on universal problems and has nothing to do with any organized religion.

Vipassana meditation can be freely practiced by everyone, at any time, in any place. Vipassana can be practiced in three ways:

❖ Be aware of actions, the body, the mind, and the heart.

❖ Be aware of the breath.
❖ Be aware of the breath at the entrance of the nostrils, when the breath goes in through the nostrils.

How to practice Vipassana meditation:

1. Choose a very quiet place for meditation.
2. Sit in a comfortable and alert position for about an hour. (It is important to choose a position that will be comfortable for this period of time. Sit with the back straight, keep eyes closed, and breathe normally.
3. Remain as still as possible, changing positions only if necessary.
4. While sitting, the primary purpose is to be aware of the rise and fall of the abdomen, caused by breathing in and out.
5. Continue to breathe normally.
6. While paying attention to the breath, practitioners may notice thoughts, judgments, emotions, and physical sensations that take their attention away from the breath, but nothing is a distraction in Vipassana. When these thoughts, judgments, emotions, and physical sensations arise, practitioners should pay attention to whatever is happening until they can go back to watching the breath.

Mind-19 ✦ Concentration Meditation

Suggested time of practice: 20 minutes

<u>How to do it:</u>

Concentration meditation is the process of bringing the mind to a single focus either within the body or an object outside the body such as a picture or a candle.

How to practice Concentration Meditation

Choose one of the following to put all your focus on it.

- ❖ Body: Find a point of concentration either inside or outside your body.
- ❖ Sound: Find a word (such as peach) or short saying (such as "I am calm") and repeat it over and over. Or find a sound either you make yourself or hear on a CD such as beating drum, chimes, or ocean waves.
- ❖ Motion: Do a repetitive motion such as a some form of rhythmic exercise (walking, running, swimming, breathing)
- ❖ Tactile: Hold a small object such as a stone, shell or beads.

Mind-20 ✦ Book Meditation

Suggested time of practice: 20 minutes

<u>How to do it:</u>

Whether you choose a text book or poetry, book meditation can be a great way to de-stress. Focusing on the words and pictures in a book can take you to other places in your mind and get you out of the 'real world' where you're stressed. It can also be used when you are studying and/or preparing for a test. You can also use this practice when you are at a lecture or seminar.

1. Sit in a comfortable chair with good back support.
2. Put the book in your lap or on a table in front of you.
3. Relax your body and your mind – getting more and more comfortable as you take a deep breath and hold it for 4 seconds and then exhale slowly.
4. Repeat deep breathing for a few minutes or however long it takes for you to feel completely relaxed both mentally and physically.
5. State the name of the book and then begin reading.
6. If at any time you notice that you are no longer relaxed, go back to deep breathing.

Mind-21 ♦ Affirmations

Suggested time of practice: Hourly

How to do it:

Affirmations such as "I am blessed with this job" and "I am calm" can seem silly but they can also really work. Based on NLP (Neuro-linguistic programming) practices, affirmations are short positive sentences that you write down on a card or piece of paper that you read over and over throughout the day. I know from experience that this can really work; I had a job where I was often getting stressed so I made a card that said "I am at peace" and put it next to my workstation so I would see it throughout the day. It took a few weeks but ultimately I did, indeed, feel more peaceful. You can use any phrase for an affirmation just make sure it is:

1. Short – no more than 7 words.
2. Focused on a single thing (you can have more than one affirmation but each one should have a single focus)
3. Written down.
4. Written in presence tense. For example, "I am happy" *not* "I will be happy" or "I am going to be happy".

Carry the card or paper with you and put it where you will see it often. Re-read it every hour.

Body practices

Body-1 ♦ Stretch

Suggested time of practice: 2-30 minutes

How to do it:

You can get rid of some of your stress by just moving. Stretching helps not only remove some stress but also helps you feel better.

How to stretch:

- ❖ Always stretch both sides of your body evenly – don't stretch one side more than the other.
- ❖ Don't overstretch – you should not feel any pain. If you do feel pain, back off; your body is not ready right now.
- ❖ Go slow. You can hold the stretch if you want for about 15 seconds.
- ❖ Do not bounce or jerk when stretching.
- ❖ Remember to breathe while stretching; never hold your breath.

Here is a simple back stretch:

1. Stand with your feet shoulder-width apart and knees bent slightly.

2. Lean forward, placing your hands on your thighs (do not put your hands on your knees).
3. Round your back so that your chest is closed and your shoulders are curved forward.
4. Then arch your back so that your chest opens and your shoulders roll back.
5. Repeat several times.

Here is a simple neck stretch:

1. Incline your head forward, but do not roll your head from side to side as this can be harmful.
2. Continue stretching your neck to the left, right, forward and back, always returning to the center first.

Repeat several times

Body-2 ✦ Massage

Suggested time of practice: 5 - 45 min2-30 minutes

How to do it:

You can get a professional massage or you can do a self-massage:

❖ Using a ball (the bigger it is, the easier it is to control) and place it between yourself and a wall. Roll the ball around using your body. You can do your back and your front just rolling it around.

❖ Use a massage stick or foam roller (available online and in stores)

❖ Use different parts of your hands – knuckles, palm, etc. and use a variety of pressures (hard, soft)

Body-3 ✦ Tai chi/ Yoga

Suggested time of practice: 10-60 minutes

How to do it:

Both Tai chi and Yoga are wonderful Eastern-based practices that require focus and movement. There are many different forms of yoga from Yin yoga which is very gentle and slow, to very complicated and physically demanding yoga. The most common types of yoga classes are listed below. Keep in mind that there is a lot of room for teacher modifications for all yoga styles except Bikram yoga. In other words, if you took a hatha yoga class at one place, the hatha yoga class at another may be completely different. There are lots of yoga videos to choose from as well.

❖ Hatha – a general term for many different types of yoga classes but generally less demanding than some other forms.
❖ Vinyasa – another general term for a variety of yoga classes but these tend to be more vigorous in style than hatha. The word Vinyasa means breath-synchronized movement.
❖ Ashtanga – a fast-paced style of yoga based on a series of poses performed in the same order each time. This yoga is physically demanding because it involves constant movement.

❖ Power Yoga – essentially Ashtanga yoga without a specific series of poses

❖ Iyengar – a slower yoga that focuses on alignment and holding poses for long periods of time. Based on yogi Ivengar, this practice often uses props such as blankets, blocks and straps to help align the body.

❖ Kundalini – this yoga focuses on breath and moving energy in the body from top to bottom. Kundalini postures are also called kriyas.

❖ Bikram- - Developed by Bikram Choudhury, this yoga is a set series of 26 different postures always done in the same order. This yoga is done in a heated room at 105 degrees and all poses are done slowly.

❖ Hot yoga- similar to Bikram yoga as it is also done in a heated room (90 degrees to 100 degrees) but the set of postures may vary.

Tai Chi is also a series of postures or positions that are done with focus and in quiet. Tai Chi, which evolved as an ancient Chinese technique of self-defense, later evolved as a form of exercise.

Tia Chi is practiced by people of all ages and is often referred to as a type of meditation with flowing movements. There are classes available in many places and videos available online and in stores.

Body-4 ♦ Reiki/Energy Healing

Suggested time of practice: 30-60 minutes

<u>How to do it:</u>

Reiki is an energy healing practice that has roots in the belief that there is energy in the universe that can help heal. Reiki can be done on humans, animals and all other living things. A Reiki practitioner uses his or her hands to move energy to help you relax and heal. Many hospitals in the United States are offering Reiki to their clients.

Reiki can be done in person or distance. Practitioners can be found in a variety of places – online, in most medium-sized cities, etc. Reiki, like other energy healing practices, can be effective in person and remotely.

There are other types of energy healing that also promote a sense of relaxation and peace. These include Quantum Touch, Healing Touch, and Reconnection.

Body-5 ♦ Acupuncture

Suggested time of practice: 45-6- minutes

<u>How to do it:</u>

Acupuncture is based on Chinese energy healing of balancing the chi in the human body. It can be used for healing specific illnesses as well as helping you de-stress. Having had many acupuncture sessions, I can say that it is not as painful as you may think. The needle is very thin and when it goes in, it only hurts for less than a second. Once all the needles are in, you will lay back and relax pain free for about 30 minutes. In that time, you will get more and more relaxed.

Acupuncturists can be found in most cities in the US.

Body-6 ♦ Deep Muscle/ Progressive Relaxation

Suggested time of practice: 10-15 minutes

<u>How to do it:</u>

Progressive muscle relaxation is a proven way to get you relaxed and free of tension and stress. It also helps you go to sleep if you do it in bed. I use it almost every night to help me relax and fall asleep. Sometimes I don't even get to my face before I've fallen asleep! To do progressive relaxation you can tighten the muscles and then relax them OR you can just relax them. After you've done it for a while, you will easily be able to relax each body part without having to tighten it first.

1. Breathe naturally – the focus is on your body not your breath.
2. Place all you attention on your feet.
3. Tighten all the muscles in your feet as hard as you can and hold then for the count of 8.
4. Then let go and allow your feet to relax.
5. Repeat this with each body part, working your way up your body to calves, upper legs, knees, etc., until your whole body is relaxed.

Body-7 ♦ Diaphragmatic Breathing

Suggested time of practice: 5-10 minutes

<u>How to do it:</u>

Deep abdominal breathing, or diaphragmatic breathing, is simply using your diaphragm to breathe, rather than using your chest.

When you breathe with your diaphragm you expand your stomach, not your chest. Your lungs will fill with air but your chest will not expand; only your stomach will expand.

Because many people carry tension in their backs, stomach or chest, deep abdominal breathing can seem to be more difficult than breathing from the chest.

Belly breathing or deep breathing is a healthier way to breathe because you actually get more oxygen when you are breathing deeply.

Diaphragmatic breathing can be difficult at first; it usually takes some practice. Here's how to practice:

1. Wear loose, comfortable clothes and have an empty stomach.
2. Lie down on the floor.
3. Put your hand on your stomach.
4. Focus on pushing your hand up when you breath in and out.
5. Try to not move your chest.

6. If you find both your chest and stomach expanding, simply practice moving only your stomach

Body-8 ✦ Aerobics

Suggested time of practice: 10-60 minutes

How to do it:

Aerobics is any exercise or movement that increases your heart rate. If you want to lose weight and burn calories, any type of aerobic exercise can help. However, to lose weight you will need to be at a high enough heart rate to require your body to access its stored energy. How high your heart rate needs to go to be considered aerobic depends on what your resting heart rate is; it's different for everyone. The easiest way to know if you are in your aerobic zone is to try to talk. If it's easy to talk then you're not in the zone. If you cannot talk at all or are gasping for air, you're in the anaerobic zone. For aerobics, you should be able to talk but it should be somewhat difficult to do so. By the way, the anaerobic zone burns less fat for fuel. However, it also burns more calories. Generally you should stay in the aerobic zone for most of the workout and, if you want, get into the breathless anaerobic zone for a short period of time. You can alternate between the two however you want. For example, walk very fast and get out of breath for 2 minutes and then walk slower for 2 minutes. This is called 'Interval training' and has been scientifically proven to burn more calories and get your heart in shape faster than steady-state aerobic exercise.

Aerobic activities include:

- ❖ Bicycling
- ❖ Hiking
- ❖ Running
- ❖ Treadmill
- ❖ Kickboxing (see Body-9)
- ❖ Dancing (see Body-22)
- ❖ Walking up and down steps
- ❖ Walking (if done quickly)
- ❖ Cross-country skiing
- ❖ Sports (See Body-23)

General aerobic video workouts are available online and in stores.

Body-9 ♦ Kickboxing

Suggested time of practice: 10-60 minutes

How to do it:

Kickboxing includes controlled kicking and punching movements that are usually very specific in type and style. It can be very easy to follow or very complicated depending on the teacher. Kickboxing can help with stress, weight loss, and overall health. However, it is recommended that you be very careful if you have knee issues as kickboxing can be hard on the knees.

Kickboxing classes are usually available at gyms and other places. There are videos available as well both online and in stores.

Body-10 ♦ Pilates

Suggested time of practice: 20 minutes

How to do it:

Pilates is named after Joseph Pilates who is credited with this method of mat exercises. Pilates involves a series of controlled movements. It can help promote focus, blood flow, and increase your flexibility.

There are live Pilates classes in most cities and there are numerous videos both online and in stores.

Body-11 ♦ Clean!

Suggested time of practice: However long it takes

How to do it:

The physical exertion of dusting, vacuuming and scrubbing reduces stress and anxiety. Yep, they have actually done studies on this.

Body-12 ◆ Garden

Suggested time of practice: 20 minutes or more

How to do it:

Working in the garden can not only release stress but it can also ground you. If you're feeling 'out of it' gardening will help get you back to yourself.

----◄€-- -----••◖◗◖•••------3◆--

Body-13 ◆ Walk the dog

Suggested time of practice: Ask the dog

How to do it:

Walking the dog is what it sounds like – get your dog or someone else's and go for a walk! You could add any of the Walking Meditations as well (see Body-16).

----◄€-- -----••◖◗◖•••------3◆--

Body-14 ◆ Slow it down

Suggested time of practice: 1-2 minutes

How to do it:

This practice is all about paying attention to your movements.

1. Starting from a standing position, walk over to a chair and sit down.

2. Close your eyes and review what you just did. Try to see each and every movement you just made.
3. Open your eyes and move as slowly as you can while reversing your movements from sitting to standing and moving back to where you were in the beginning of the exercise.
4. Close your eyes again, and review how different it felt to go as slow as possible in your movements.
5. Repeat if you want or do the same with different movements.

Body-15 ♦ Walking Meditation

Suggested time of practice: 20 minutes

How to do it:

Walking as a meditative practice is an efficient and healthy way to promote relaxation. This technique can be used in a beautiful forest, on the beach, or even in the mall

To perform a walking meditation, you can start by focusing first on the footfall as a whole, or you can start with the left foot and begin walking slowly while synchronizing the breathing in and out with each step. Walking meditation may be practiced at any pace.

An alternative is:

Walk as you normally do but synchronize your breaths with your arms - as one arm goes forward, breathe in, as the other goes forward, breathe out. Start out slowly and increase your speed as you get into the rhythm. Focus all your attention on breathing along with your arm movements.

Body-16 ♦ Walking the Labyrinth

Suggested time of practice: 20 minutes

<u>How to do it:</u>

Walking a labyrinth is another form of walking meditation. It combines the actions of the body, mind, and spirit with the imagery of a circle and spiral to create a purposeful path. An ancient activity, labyrinth walking is reemerging in churches, schools, parks, and medical centers, where staff, clients, and families walk the labyrinth to reduce stress, relax, and deal with loss and grief.

The meditative response to walking a labyrinth is both formal and ritualistic. It includes three phases:

- ❖ **Releasing** occurs during the walk as the practitioner empties the mind and repeats a word, chant, or prayer.
- ❖ **Receiving** occurs when the walker reaches the center of the labyrinth (sitting or standing while inviting an opening to healing, connection, and renewal).
- ❖ **Returning** involves retracing one's steps in the opposite direction.

Walkers may experience a change of energy in mind, body, and spirit. The average labyrinth walk is about 20 minutes, and the intention is to evoke physiological, affective, and spiritual outcomes.

--------◄----------►-◎-◄---►----3◄--

Body-17 ✦ Whirling Dervishes Sufi Meditation

Suggested time of practice: 20 minutes

How to do it:

Sufi paths to oneness call for different meditation techniques. The two central practices of the Naqshbandi path, for example, are the silent *dhikr* (remembrance of God) and the silent *zikr* (meditation of the heart).

In Sufi meditative practice, the meditator believes that there is no god but God and the way to purity is by a constant remembrance of God. Remembrance of God involves repeating His name, thus purifying the seeker's mind and opening the heart to Him. As is common to most meditation systems, the goal of zikr is to overcome the mind's natural state of carelessness and inattention. Whirling dervishes are a group of Sufi Muslims who use dancing (whirling and spinning) as a form of meditation and as a way to reach a spiritual state of mind.

The word *dervish* comes from the root word "dar," meaning door, and "vish," meaning contemplation or meditation.

Whirling is common among Sufis around the world. Whirling dervishes are comprised of the followers of a man called Rumi, born between 1200 and 1207. Rumi became a famous

Sufi scholar, a dervish, and a poet. His books can be found in most every bookstore and library in the US.

When the whirling dervishes turn in circles, they are in a state of meditative prayer. As they spin, they believe there is a point in the center of their being that allows the heavens and the universe to join in the dance.

They spin in a way that they believe will make the light of God ascend to the earth when their right hand is turned upward pointing to the heavens and their left hand is pointed downward, which brings the light down into the world.

Body-18 ♦ Rocking

Suggested time of practice: 20 minutes or more

How to do it:

Simply rocking in a rocking chair can reduce your stress levels if you add daydreaming while you are rocking, you will reduce stress even quicker and easier. Daydreaming is also recommended in the Mind practices. It is so powerful. Studies have shown that daydreaming has the same brain wave patterns as those induced when meditating.

Body-19 ♦ Vibrational and Sound Meditation

Suggested time of practice: 20 minutes

How to do it:

Vibrational and sound meditations are excellent techniques for those who find it difficult to concentrate. Taoists often use a mantra* of *Who, Shoe, Foo, Way,* or *She,* which improves concentration and strengthens the body. Each sound corresponds to an internal organ, and the energy vibration from the sound is believed to help heal that organ.

*A mantra is a word or sound that serves as a focal point for certain types of meditation. In certain religious groups, a mantra is used to achieve spiritual transformation. In psychology, mantras may be used to achieve a hypnotic trance, or simply to quickly reach a point of deep relaxation

Meditation with sound uses mantras, chanting, singing bowls, drums, or CDs to incorporate sound vibrations in the promotion of a meditative state of mind.

How to practice Vibrational and Sound Meditation

You can choose which type of modality to use:

❖ **Mantras** involve synchronizing the breathing with the silent repetition of a sound, word, or phrase (such as sacred Sanskrit syllables and words like "om"). Mantras are used in numerous practices and can be added to others. The word **Mantra** is from Sanskrit and means "sacred utterance" although the term is now commonly used for any repetition of a syllable, word, or group of words repeated numerous times. The terms Mantra and Chanting have come to be somewhat interchangeable. **Chanting** involves repeating certain words or sounds aloud.

- ❖ **Singing bowls,** usually made of a unique alloy or quartz crystal, are rubbed or struck with a wooden stick to create soothing sounds that invoke a meditative state.
- ❖ **Drums** are beaten in rhythm with the breath or heartbeat to create a deep meditative state.

CDs of music, nature sounds, or meditation instructions can help create a relaxed meditative state.

Body-20 ♦ A Toast!

Suggested time of practice: 2 minutes

<u>How to do it:</u>

Sometimes you just need to get a little physical (and a little alcohol) to get rid of your stress. This practice is for those over legal drinking age. You will also need to have a broom and dustbin since you will be making a mess!

In Russia and other European countries sometimes when they celebrate they throw their glass into a fireplace after they've drunk from the glass. This practice is quick, easy, and fun. To bring a bit of play to your de-stressing, consider using this European practice to get rid of your stress.

There are numerous toasts that can be used; the easiest is "Za vas!" (zah VAHS) if you want to be 'official' about it. You could say anything you want, though. Maybe "Goodbye stress!" or "To Calmness!"

I am not recommending that you do this on a regular basis or that you drink a lot of alcohol and, in fact, you could do this with water. It's the physical act of toasting and breaking the glass that are the essential actions here as it can be freeing to release your stress this way. Feel free to modify this in any way you want.

1. Get a glass that you don't care about.
2. Fill the glass with alcohol of your choice (or any other liquid.)
3. After you've drunk the liquid, yell "ZA VAS!" And throw the class into the fireplace or other safe place. Alternately you could break the glass with your feet.

Body-21 ♦ Gum

Suggested time of practice: 15 Minutes

<u>How to do it:</u>

Chewing gum can help work out some of that stress that you're holding. I've found it to be very helpful in stop-and-go traffic. I just pop a couple pieces of gum in my mouth and chew away my stress.

Get yourself a couple pieces of gum and chew the heck out of it. Blow bubbles if you can (if you're alone, just go for it!).

Body-22 ♦ Dance

Suggested time of practice: 5-60 minutes

<u>How to do it:</u>

Dancing can be a great way to get rid of stress! There are lots of types of dance to choose from:

- ❖ Hip-hop and other street dancing
- ❖ Bollywood
- ❖ Ballroom
- ❖ Jazz
- ❖ Hula
- ❖ Country line dancing
- ❖ Folk
- ❖ Disco

You could 'just dance' (Freestyle) or you could find a class. There are also many videos available online and in stores as well. You could also go to a club and dance the night away. That would surely relieve some stress! (See also Body-8)

───────────

Body-23 ♦ Sports

Suggested time of practice: 5-60 minutes

<u>How to do it:</u>

There are so many different sports to choose from… you could join a team or shoot some baskets with a friend. Here are a few to consider:

- ❖ Tag games

- ❖ Swimming
- ❖ Archery
- ❖ Motorcycle racing
- ❖ Card games
- ❖ Racket ball
- ❖ Fishing
- ❖ Horseback riding
- ❖ Ice Skating
- ❖ Sailing
- ❖ Gymnastics
- ❖ Golfing
- ❖ Climbing

(See also Body-8)

Spiritual practices

Spirit-1 ♦ Mudra & Meditation

Suggested time of practice: 20 minutes

<u>*How to do it:*</u>

A mudra is an Eastern term for a hand gesture or body movement that repeats an idea or state of mind. The most common mudra is the one you see Buddha doing – cross-legged with his palm facing up and his index finger and thumb touching. This position is called the jnana mudra. It symbolizes opening the heart to the wisdom of heaven. Another common mudra is the prayer mudra, atmanjali, with the palms together and fingers pointed upward in the familiar gesture of prayer. The prayer mudra symbolizes communication with the divine. For this practice,

1. Sit in a comfortable position.
2. Select a point of focus (a candle works nicely.)
3. Slowly bring your hands into one of the mudras described above.
4. Sit in this position for concentrating on the point of focus,

Spirit-2 ✦ Give it to Spirit

Suggested time of practice: 10 minutes

How to do it:

When you give your worries, stresses, and concerns to Spirit, you get out of your own way and allow Spirit to help. All you have to do is ask. It's simple but we get so busy and so bogged down by what's going on around us that we forget this simple, yet very effective, practice. You may want to write on a card something like "Spirit is there for me, all I have to do is ask" and carry it with you to remind yourself to ask for help.

Spirit-3 ✦ Heaven on Earth

Suggested time of practice: 10 minutes

How to do it:

Sometimes when you are feeling stressed, it's because you have been focusing on the negative and on what is happening to you as 'wrong'. It may be a time when, rather than acting, you need to stop and go to your quiet, spiritual place and reach out for Spirit's hand. It is those who care that worry. Those who don't care don't worry or get stressed. Sometimes the very fact that you are stressed is a very good thing because it means you care, just as you should. There will be times when you need to shield yourself from the negativity. Call on Spirit to walk with you through the darkness and back into the light. This too will pass. If you walk with Spirit, you will find Heaven on Earth.

Spirit-4 ✦ Spiritual Affirmations

Suggested time of practice: Hourly reminders

How to do it:

Our lives are very busy and when we get stressed it's easy to forget what really matters. Affirmations are a great way to remind ourselves. Here are some suggestions:

> God is my source.
> Jesus is my guide.
> Buddha is my teacher.
> Spirit is here now.
> Love is all that matters.

You can use any phrase for an affirmation just make sure it is:

- ❖ Short – no more than 7 words.
- ❖ Focused on a single thing. (You can have more than one affirmation but each one should have a single focus.)
- ❖ Written down.
- ❖ Written in present test.

Carry the card or paper with you and put it where you will see it often.

Spirit-5 ◆ Prayer

Suggested time of practice: As desired

How to do it:

This practice is simple. In whatever way you pray to Spirit, do it. You may want to write your prayers down as well because the act of writing it down helps you get physically involved as well. Also, spoken prayer has been shown to be more effective than silent prayer. Also, try to focus the prayer by being specific and visualizing what you are praying for to enhance the prayer.

Spirit-6 ◆ Forgive

Suggested time of practice: 20 minutes

How to do it:

Forgiveness can be a Mind or a Spirit practice but for me it is more spiritual because it includes a spiritual aspect. I believe that when we forgive someone for something they did to us, we need to get beyond simply saying that we forgive them.

1. See the person as a human just like you. They are doing the best they can with what they know.
2. Ask yourself, what have I learned from this experience? Even if you don't know right now, it will most likely show up at some point in your life that what they 'did to you' actually helped you learn something about yourself and others.
3. What did they teach you?

I believe that each of us is here to learn lessons and those who help us learn a lesson are sent by Spirit to do so. True forgiveness actually brings you to a place where you can be grateful for what happened. Don't get me wrong, what happened doesn't go away – depending on what the issue is, you may remember and be affected by it for the rest of your life since it is imprinted in you. But, how much it affects you will lessen as time goes by. There will be times that something happens and you are back where you were before forgiving but that's OK. Just remind yourself of the good that came out of the situation. Ask Spirit to remind you if you can't remember. There is a peace that comes from going through this process and a stronger connection to Spirit.

Spirit-7 ♦ Gratitude

Suggested time of practice: 10 minutes

<u>How to do it:</u>

Make a gratitude list. Every day add to your list and re-read your list. This practice reminds you that Spirit is with you and guiding you. Gratitude is essentially thanking Spirit. Reminding yourself daily of all the wonderful things Spirit has brought to your life helps you be less stressed as you focus on the positive rather than the negative.

Spirit-8 ♦ Hindu Meditation

Suggested time of practice: 20 minutes

How to do it:

As the oldest known religion in the world to practice meditation, Hinduism has an extensive focus on meditation as a main component of its religious practice. Though the means may differ in each type of meditation states, they all "seek to transcend duality in union." They see the center of duality as within the mind, in the separation between the mechanisms of awareness and their object. To transcend duality, the seeker must enter a state where the gap between the mind and the object exists. Hindu meditation involves listening, attentively and in silence to the voice of the Absolute within. In the deepest depths of Hindu meditation, all is silent.

There are several types of meditation in Hinduism, including the following practices. Please note that these yoga practices are done sitting; there are moving yoga practices in the Body Practices section (see Body-3).

- ❖ **Japa yoga:** A mantra (See Body-20) or divine name is chanted or repeated softly or silently during this practice.
- ❖ **Raja yoga:** Also known as Ashtanga yoga, this type of yoga deals with the cultivation of the mind with the goal of achieving liberation.
- ❖ **Vedanta yoga** (a form of Jnana yoga): Its name means "the culmination of knowledge," based on the ancient scriptures of the Upanishads (a sacred religious text in Hinduism). The scriptures reveal the types of meditation used in Vedanta.

Surat shabd yoga: This type of meditation seeks union with the Divine, which is seen as creative energy embodied in sound.

Spirit-9 ♦ Tibetan Buddhism

Suggested time of practice: 20 minutes

<u>How to do it:</u>

In this form of meditative practice, the meditator realizes three moral precepts—known as the triple refuge of Buddha, Dharma, and Sangha—as internal realities. The Tibetan Buddhist meditator follows three principles:

❖ **Sila:** Vowing to practice "upright" (moral and ethical) behavior
❖ **Samadhi:** Fixing the mind on one object to develop "one-pointedness" (a state of being completely focused)
❖ **Vipassana:** Seeing things as they really are (self-purification and self-observation)

In Tibetan Buddhism, the path to enlightenment is achieved through compassion, altruistic thought, and the perfect view (faith in the teachings of Buddha). This positive transformation is the practice of the "three trainings":

❖ **Renunciation,** or the determination to be free from the prison-like realms of existence (a method that supports the infinite potential for life to express itself and its interconnectedness to the environment and to transcend suffering).

❖ **The awakening mind or *bodhichitta*,** an altruistic wish to achieve Buddhahood for the sake of all sentient beings

❖ **Wisdom,** or realizing emptiness (grasping the true nature of reality)

It is difficult to understand the true nature of Tibetan Buddhism without participating in its practices. Specific methods in Tibetan Buddhist meditation are transmitted only from teacher (guru) to student in centuries-old teaching lineages. Most monks meditate in a traditional Buddhist posture but are also likely to chant or participate in group liturgies to awaken the true nature of the mind.

There are numerous Tibetan temples in the US and often they welcome anyone who wishes to join in meditation. There are also meditations available online for download and streaming audio. There are specific meditations available for each of the principles: ***Sila, Samadhi*** and ***Vipassana*** (which is included in the Mind Practice section – Mind-16).

--- ◄┊ ─────── ┅►◄●►◄┅ ── ┊► ──

Spirit-10 ♦ Centering Prayer Meditation

Suggested time of practice: 20 minutes

How to do it:

Centering prayer meditation is considered a way of having a relationship with God (and the living Christ) and a discipline to help foster that relationship.

Because of its Christian foundation, the source of centering prayer meditation is the trinity—the Father, the Son, and the

Holy Spirit. Centering prayer meditation is considered a form of prayer but it is not meant to replace other forms of prayer.

The focus is on establishing a deep and personal connection with God through silence and stillness. As with other meditations, Centering Prayer includes recognizing any thoughts that come up and letting them go. Do not focus on them or allow them to distract you, simply turn your mind back to God.

How to practice Centering Prayer meditation:
The seven steps to practice centering prayer meditation include the following:

- ❖ **Silence:** Consenting to God's presence (what Jesus calls the Kingdom of God within and among us)
- ❖ **Solitude:** A place of oneness that flows from inner silence
- ❖ **Solidarity:** The awareness of increasing oneness with God, with the entire human family, and with all creation
- ❖ **Service:** Following the inspirations of the Spirit not only during the time of formal prayer but in the details of everyday life; God in us serving God in others
- ❖ **Stillness:** The experience of God's presence beyond rational concepts, beyond preoccupation with one's personal thoughts and desires
- ❖ **Simplicity:** The integration of contemplation and action (the capacity to live in the midst of duality—the ups and downs of daily life—without losing the non-dual perspective
- ❖ **Surrender:** The total gift of self to God (a movement from union to unity)

Spirit-11 ♦ Zen Meditation

Suggested time of practice: 20 minutes

<u>How to do it:</u>

Zen philosophy is more similar to Taoism than other forms of Buddhism. For example, in Zen Buddhist schools of thought, Zen philosophy includes the following four characteristics

- ❖ Additional information beyond what is written in the Buddhist scriptures (something **beyond** the words of any teacher or the **scriptures** of any dogma)
- ❖ Detachment from the ancient texts
- ❖ Realization about the absolute purity of the mind
- ❖ Contemplation of one's own nature to obtain the state of the Buddha (an everlasting **state** of great joy and peace called nirvana)

Zen philosophy teaches that awakening must be experienced in all of life's activities, which are symbolized by the four postures of walking, standing, sitting, and lying which forms a bridge between meditation and everyday life. In Zen philosophy, walking, standing, sitting, and lying are spiritual postures, but not all postures are typically meditation postures. Sitting is the most common posture in life because it is the most stable, it grounds one to the earth, and it is the core posture in Zen meditation.

In Zen, seated meditation is called **zazen.** In zazen, the meditator's goal is to let go of all external distractions, return to the original stillness within the self, and discover the essence of who he or she truly is. In the sitting posture, the meditator aims for a heightened state of concentrated awareness with no primary objective. The meditator sits, with open eyes, often looking down so the eyes are only partly open.

The full lotus position (sitting cross-legged with the feet pressed into the groin) and the half lotus position (sitting cross-legged with the feet pressed into the fold of the leg) are the preferred ways of creating a stable foundation. Sitting cushions, known as zafus, help support the body to maintain the correct posture.

The breathing that accompanies the sitting posture is open and relaxed and often newcomers are recommended to count the breaths to 100 and then back down to 1.

------◆------◆◆◆------◆------

Spirit12- ✦ Taoist Meditation

Suggested time of practice: 20 minutes

How to do it:

One of the most ancient Eastern traditions, Taoism is becoming increasingly popular in the modern West, partly because Taoism is scientific yet also humanistic and spiritual. Taoism is a science because it is based upon a detailed understanding of underlying physical, chemical, biological, mathematical, psychological, and political theories and laws.

Taoist meditation methods share traits in common with Hindu and Buddhist meditation, but the Taoist way is less abstract than the contemplative traditions of Hindu and Buddhist meditation. Taoist meditation involves the generation, transformation, and circulation of internal energy.

Tao is translated in the English language as "the way." The following are characteristics of Tao.

❖ Taoism is a way of life and a path toward the ultimate truth.

❖ For some, Taoism is a religion; for others, it is a philosophy of life; and for others, it is a science that helps them understand the great cosmos.

❖ Tao can be described as "everything we can conceive and can't conceive with our limited mind. It is everything definable and indefinable. It is both physical and nonphysical. It has to be understood through introspection and realization of a greater consciousness".

❖ Taoism can be practiced within the framework of other world religions or without any religious framework.

Taoism includes various meditative and contemplative traditions. The principles are described in the I Ching, Tao Te Ching, Chuang Tzu, and Tao Tsang, among other texts.

Taoists believe that their lives are not predetermined, so they emphasize cultivating both the spirit and the physical body. They use meditation to clear what they call the mental space (an inner area of the mind) and to allow the meditator to return to the stage known as Wu-chi, or the void. The clearing out of the mental space can be compared to cleaning out a room full of cluttered possessions.

While Taoist techniques emphasize the art of harmonizing the breath to reach higher states, the various Tao schools of meditation teach different methods. The following seven techniques of meditation are some of those methods.

- ❖ **Concentration:** Concentration can be either internal (such as concentrating on one point in the body about 2 inches below the navel and 1.5 inches inside the body) or external (such as focusing on an object outside the body, such as a picture).

- ❖ **Contemplation:** Contemplation requires a more advanced use of the imagination than concentration requires. One example is experiencing thoughts as individual bubbles rising through the water of the inner self, allowing the meditator to regulate the timing of thoughts (bubbles) and experience each thought as an individual entity.

- ❖ **Counting the breath:** Probably the easiest meditation technique, counting the breath can be practiced by anyone. A breath is a complete cycle of inhalation and exhalation. Any number of breaths can be counted; the important thing is to think only of the counting and the breath. If thoughts disturb this technique, just refocus on the breath.

- ❖ **Meditation of self-inquiry:** A difficult form of meditation, this type involves asking the mind to ask itself who it really is. Each answer (e.g., a family member, a name, a feeling) must be examined and then rejected in search of a clearer answer as the meditator continues to ask, "Who is my inner self?"

- ❖ **Unstructured meditation:** This type has no structure or technique. The mind chooses an image or concept and actively examines and contemplates it. Interfering thoughts are explored and discarded.

- ❖ **Use of a sound or mantra:** This is an excellent technique for those who find it difficult to concentrate. Taoists may use a mantra of *Who, Shoe, Foo, Way, Chemmy, She,* which improves concentration and strengthens the body through the correspondence of each sound with an internal organ.

Movement: An example of movement meditation is Tai Chi During this type of meditation, practitioners must give up all thoughts and become tranquil as they move through a series of specific poses.

Spirit-13 ✦ Christian Meditation

Suggested time of practice: 20 minutes

How to do it:

Christian meditation is a form of prayer and contemplative reflection that goes back to the time of Jesus and the Jewish tradition. The first Christian monks sought isolation to commune with God, free of worldly distractions. Although they used the teachings of Jesus as their inspiration, the monks used meditative techniques that were similar to those from the East. They meditated by verbally or silently repeating a single phrase from the Scriptures, the Christian equivalent of a mantra (See Body-20).

The term *centering prayer,* an aspect of Christian meditation, is a new term introduced in the 20th century. Centering prayer is best described as a receptive method of meditation. Inspired by the acclaimed Catholic spiritual writer Thomas Merton, centering prayer in its purity seeks nothing for the meditator.

The meditator seeks simply and totally to give himself or herself to the Divine.

1. Sit in a relaxed position with your eyes closed.
2. Choose to be in a state of mind in which you place your faith and love in God.
3. Choose a sacred word (such as *God, peace, love, nature*) as your intention to consent to have God's presence and action within you.
4. Be aware of your thoughts and keep gently returning to your sacred word.
5. At the end of your prayer period, remain in silence with your eyes closed for a couple of minutes.

To help you develop a one-on-one relationship with God the following practices are suggested:

- ❖ **Know what you want:** Focus on what you want, not on what you don't want.
- ❖ **Choose to be happy:** Happiness is a **thought** in the now and is independent of people, things, or circumstances.
- ❖ **Play a game of make-believe:** Co-create your own destiny with the power of your thoughts.
- ❖ **Use your powers for good:** Your enlightened presence can uplift the energy of your environment.
- ❖ **Life is easy:** You can make your life complicated or choose to make it simple.
- ❖ **You get to know only the next step:** Enjoy the precise moment of your journey.
- ❖ **Work from within your core of creativity:** Contribute your gifts and talents to the rest of humanity, and you will find an unlimited supply of possibilities for yourself.

- ❖ **Return to the basics:** Eat healthily, exercise daily, drink plenty of water, get enough sleep, and maintain a clean and organized home.
- ❖ **Know that you are loved:** God loves you.
- ❖ **There is only plan A:** You can have the life you choose to have.
- ❖ **Have a theme song:** Singing uplifts the spirit; find your own theme song that energizes you.

Meditations include some of the same practices as other forms of meditation, such as praying, reading, giving thanks, creating good thoughts, journaling, and listening to music.

Spirit-14 ♦ Sufi Meditation

Suggested time of practice: 20 minutes

How to do it:

Sufi meditation is synonymous with the term "noble connection," which has always been a central practice of Islamic spirituality, or Sufism. Sufis are members of the mystical, ascetic branch of Islam. Sufism is a path of love and the ancient wisdom of the heart. Sufi meditation seeks to fuse the individual back into oneness with the Universal Reality. Sufi meditation is one way individuals detach themselves from the "false" world and immerse themselves in reality (the world that lies behind the realm of the current world, considered an illusion).

In the Sufi tradition, saints are those who have overcome their lower nature, and meditation is essential for those who seek to escape their lower natures and purify their hearts. The Sufi is on a journey back to the Divine and this journey takes place within the heart.

Sufis believe that meditation is essential to purify the heart, and they aim for a total and permanent purity. Sufi meditation takes the meditator from a world of duality to a world of oneness within the heart. Sufi meditation is not limited by time, place, or form.

In Sufi tradition, the mind is purified and disciplined through the continual practice of meditation. The first step is learning to listen inwardly and the second stop is learning to be silent.

In Sufi meditative practice, the meditator believes that there is no god but God and the way to purity is by a constant remembrance of God. Remembrance of God involves repeating His name, thus purifying the seeker's mind and opening the heart to Him. As is common to most meditation systems, the goal is to overcome the mind's natural state of carelessness and inattention.

Also see Whirling dervish (Body-18)

Spirit-15 ♦ Jewish Meditation

Suggested time of practice: 20 minutes

<u>How to do it:</u>

Traditional Jewish meditation uses words, images, and symbols from Jewish observances, such as prayer and Torah study.

Jewish meditation goes back thousands of years and is found in major Jewish texts in every period from biblical to the post-modern times.

Throughout history, Jewish meditation has grown and changed, absorbing elements from other traditions such as Sufism, Buddhism, and Gnosticism. It also absorbed aspects of mainstream Judaism, which includes a strong tradition of meditation and mysticism. Jewish mysticism seeks to answer the basic questions asked by man for thousands of years such as, "What is the nature of God?" "What is the meaning of creation?" and "Why is there both good and evil?"

Jewish meditation includes many of the practices listed in this book such as Visualization, Contemplation, Mantra's, and Mindfulness. The focus for Jewish meditators is God and may include the use of a biblical verse as the focus of the meditation.

An additional meditation that is not found in many other practices is the Oral Conversation which includes three important characteristics:

❖ It is a verbal type of meditation that involves the use of words in thought or speech as a way of focusing rather than the use of images on which to focus.
❖ It is inner directed.
❖ It is unstructured and the meditator has no preconceived notion of which direction the meditation will take.

The mystical side of Judaism is the Kabbalah. There are various formats for Kabbala meditation. Here is one.

1. Light a candle and sandalwood incense.

2. Wear loose, comfortable clothes.
3. Turn off all electric devices that will distract you.
4. Sit in an upright position so your back is perfectly straight.
5. Touch your first finger with your thumb finder on each hand.
6. Ring a bell and say "This temple is now open."
7. Take 3 deep breathes and hold for 3 seconds and then release.
8. Count down from 30 to 1.
9. Say out loud "I am a completion and piece of the puzzle connected to Source."
10. Sit, allowing thoughts to come and go.
11. When 20 minutes is up, finish the meditation with saying out loud "I AM that I AM."

Keep a pad and pen nearby to write down ideas and insights that come to you after the meditation is done.

Spirit-16 ♦ Simplify

Suggested time of practice: 20 minutes

How to do it:

Simplifying your lifestyle can help you feel not only less stress, but also help you get more done. Before you can simplify, you need to know what your goals are. To begin simplifying your life:

1. Write down your goals – what you want to accomplish in each area of your life: work, family, etc.

2. Rank your goals from the most important to the least important.
3. Write down your spiritual goals and prioritize them as well.
4. Create a single list with the three most important items, including your spiritual goals.
5. Ask yourself how much time am I spending on my top three goals?
6. Ask yourself: What am I doing now that is not contributing to my goals? What do I spend my time doing that isn't moving me forward?
7. Remind yourself often of your list and that focusing on what's important is essential for peace of mind – it is OK to let less important things fall to the wayside. Ask Spirit to help you with any possible guilt you feel by not doing everything on your list at once; all goals will be reached at some point. Say" "Right now I am focusing on_____."

This practice can be profound. Most of us don't stop and really think about what goals are important to us much less prioritize them. If you do this every month or so, you will also see how having this list helps you get more done.

--◄---------►(●)◄--------3►--

Spirit-17- ♦ Ask and Listen

Suggested time of practice: 20 minutes

<u>How to do it:</u>

There is a still, small voice inside of us that is speaking, but we don't always listen. The art of spirituality is having one ear heeding our duties on earth and the other on the inner voice of wisdom.

That inner voice can come to you as a direction from your Higher Self or as a signal from your soul. It could be a gentle nudge from an Angel. Either way, if you listen to it you will find peace, love, and contentment. It can provide you with inner guidance and direction if you just ask and then listen for the answer. The more you listen to your inner voice, the better you will get at it.

Take a chance and try it. Ask Spirit for help with something and be listening for the answer. It will come but you need to listen. When you get the answer, follow it. Do as you feel guided and you'll see that the answer provided the advice. Whether it is something as small and seemingly insignificant as a new pair of shoes for that super special outing or something as big as how to get along with your boss, the answers are all there if you ask and listen.

If you prefer to do a more formal version of asking and listening, you can do a visualization:

1. Close your eyes and see yourself entering a secret chamber where you come face-to-face with your Higher Self/God/Inner Wisdom/Spirit.
2. Say the following prayer:
   a. I am open to hear, sense, and feel, perceive the inner wisdom that is mine to receive. Show me how to listen with an open heart and how to use the wisdom you give me.
3. Listen for the answer in whichever way it comes. It could be an inner knowing, an unexpected phone call, something someone suddenly says, etc.

4. With heartfelt gratitude, thank Spirit and your Higher Self for the answers you received.

------◦------

Spirit-18 ✦ Sacred Space

Suggested time of practice: 20 minutes

<u>How to do it:</u>

Sacred space can help you make a connection with Spirit more easily. You can do this simply and easily by setting up your personal altar in your home, even if it is in a corner of the bedroom.

You can place on the altar whatever inspires or helps you feel a connection with Spirit. It may be pictures, statues, inspirational sayings, shells, crystals, etc. This altar is where you go to 'alter' yourself. This is where you can go and feel the love and acceptance of Spirit. This is your inner sanctuary where you can:

❖ Pray (see Spirit-5)
❖ Have a morning conversation with Spirit
❖ Have a private ceremony

Just relax and let the love of Spirit fill you.

------◦------

Spirit-19 ♦ Visualization Meditation

Suggested time of practice: 20 minutes

How to do it:

Visualization is any meditation where you visualize something. It is a form of meditation in which you use your imagination to relax your body, mind, and spirit. Visualization is seeing with your mind.

Visualization can change your frame of mind. Your thoughts and feelings project energy and attract energy of a similar nature. When you do a visualization practice it can change your thoughts and feelings so you feel more peaceful.

When you begin visualizing as a form of meditation, start with a very basic visualization such as the ocean, or a peaceful meadow. Use something that you've seen, a place you've actually been where you felt calm and peaceful. Once you can do that and stay in that place for ten minutes or so, you are ready for a longer visualization such as the one below. There are lots and lots of visualizations available online. It may be easier for you to listen to one rather than read and try to remember what you are supposed to do. The visualization below is fairly simple so you can remember it when you are mediating.

Contacting with Spirit visualization
1. Get into a comfortable position either laying down or sitting in a chair that supports you back.
2. Close your eyes and take some long, deep breaths, slowly breathing in and then out.

3. Now imagine you are in a beautiful forest. The trees are so tall they touch the sky. You can see and smell the pine trees all around you.
4. You see a path in front of you. A grassy path that goes deeper into the forest.
5. You walk down the path, following it as you get deeper and deeper into the forest.
6. The path widens and you see a small building up ahead.
7. You walk to the building and into it.
8. You look around the large room that you are standing in and see things that you know and that you love. Take some time to see everything that is in the room. Look around and make note of how you are feeling comforted by the things you see.
9. You see a large, comfortable chair in front of you and walk to it and sit down.
10. As you sit in the chair, you realize that you feel completely comfortable and safe.
11. You feel a deep, quiet inside yourself.
12. You feel Spirit all around you, comforting and loving you.
13. You want to ask Spirit a question and you do so. (Ask your question now).
14. You get an answer from Spirit and thank Spirit for the answer. You tell yourself that you will remember your question and Spirit's answer after you have left this wonderful place.
15. You sit with Spirit for a little while and bask in the peace and love you feel.
16. When you are ready, you get out of the chair and walk toward the door. You know that you can come back to this place anytime you want.
17. You slowly follow the path back to the forest where you started.

18. You open your eyes slowly and return to the room.

You may choose to write down your question and answer at this time.

--◆§·-- -----◆·•◆(●)◆•·•----- --◈◆--

Spirit-20 ◆ Labyrinth Meditation

Suggested time of practice: 20 minutes

<u>How to do it:</u>

Walking a labyrinth is also described in Body-16. I include it here as well because it can be a very effective spiritual practice as well if you focus on spirit and a short word, chant or prayer with every step. The directions from Body-16 are below.

Walking a labyrinth is another form of walking meditation. It combines the actions of the body, mind, and spirit with the imagery of a circle and spiral to create a purposeful path. An ancient activity, labyrinth walking is reemerging in churches, schools, parks, and medical centers, where staff, clients, and families walk the labyrinth to reduce stress, relax, and deal with loss and grief.

The meditative response to walking a labyrinth is both formal and ritualistic. It includes three phases:

- ❖ **Releasing** occurs during the walk as the practitioner empties the mind and repeats a word, chant, or prayer.
- ❖ **Receiving** occurs when the walker reaches the center of the labyrinth (sitting or standing while inviting an opening to healing, connection, and renewal).

❖ **Returning** involves retracing one's steps in the opposite direction.

Walkers may experience a change of energy in mind, body, and spirit. The average labyrinth walk is about 20 minutes, and the intention is to evoke physiological, affective, and spiritual outcomes.

Conclusion
How to Live a (mostly)
Stress-Free Life

❖ Accept That You Are Human
You are NOT perfect, superman or superwoman, everything to everyone, or here to make huge, miraculous changes in the world in anyone except yourself. You are not capable of being, doing, or acting perfectly. No human being is.

❖ Understand That You Have ALL The Control And NONE Of The Control
You can control all of *your* actions and take responsibility for them but none of the control of others' actions or responsibilities. Accepting responsibility for your actions and words is very empowering. Letting others have responsibility for their own words and actions is empowering for them.

❖ Know That Everything Happens For A Reason But You May Never Know Why
There are things that happen, ways people react, and jobs that you don't get. You may never know why. It's natural to want to know why but it's not always possible.

❖ Take Chances But Only Ones That You Actually Have A Chance Of Succeeding At
Know your limits and admit them to yourself and others. Know when you can choose to act and not choose to act by trusting your intuition to guide you to the next succeed-able challenge.

❖ Laugh More
Learn to laugh at yourself and at 'the situation'. There is always humor in being human, so why not enjoy our foibles? We aren't perfect so let's lighten up and laugh at our silly selves sometimes.

❖ Respect Yourself And Every Living Thing On The Planet
We all deserve to be here equally. Everything is part of the Universe and no one is better or more special than anyone else. You are a part of All-That-Is. As part of All-That-Is, you are able to make wonderfully miraculous changes one person at a time (starting with yourself). You are connected to everyone and everything else.

❖ Trust Your Intuition
If you trust your intuition you will be in the flow. The universe has a flow to it and as long as you stay with the flow of it, you will know what to do and when.